For *The Flame Bearers*

"Full of surprise and susp~~~ ~~~ ~~~~~~~~~ ~~ traditional knowledge that shines on every page gives the book its depth and humor."

—Anne Roiphe, *New York Times Book Review*

"Immensely compelling ... lyrical ... Chernin provides a dreamlike setting for events, a quality found in the works of Gabriel Garcia Marquez and Isaac Bashevis Singer."

—The *San Francisco Chronicle*

"Worshippers of the Mother will welcome Chernin's bold first novel ... The flashback parts are told by the old woman in a voice as engaging as those in Isaac Bashevis Singer's tales of villages, bathhouses, and possession ... In all, Chernin keeps us interested through her energetic recreation of the past."

—*Kirkus Review*

"Certainly women have been reading books, from Scripture to the novels of Philip Roth, in which they play the supporting role while God talks with the men. *The Flame Bearers* will be read with delight by those who enjoy good ideological revenge, a turning of the tables."

—*New York Times Book Review*

For *In My Mother's House*

"What a fascinating, rich, beautiful book: an illumination of our times—humanly, politically—interwoven with a profound portrayal of the ever-changing, deepening relationship between mother, daughter, and eventually granddaughter. A book that will be an American resource."

—Tillie Olsen

"*In My Mother's House* adds a triumphant dimension to the body of [mother-daughter] literature. Triumphant not only because it is profoundly moving and splendidly written, but also because Rose and Kim Chernin achieve a rare level of communication and understanding."

—Ann Martin-Leff, *New Directions for Women*

"This brave and thoughtful memoir is an artistic triumph that brings rich characters to life, while quickening the feelings that lie at the heart of every family's struggle."
—Helen Mayer, *Newsday*

"We have this book because Kim Chernin longed to know her mother, 'save' an important life, and communicate her to the next generation (as well as the rest of us) ... There are stories in this book that I will never forget."
—Grace Paley, author of *The Little Disturbances of Man* and *Enormous Changes at the Last Minute*

"Read *In My Mother's House* to know what it was like on the left or as a teenage girl in the fifties, but read it more for its dazzling literary structure, its passionate intelligence, and its ferocious clarity."
—Louise Bernikow, author of *The World Split Open* and *Among Women*

For *In My Father's Garden*

"*[In My Father's Garden]* is the basis for a new 'spiritual politics'—for which, in her honest, fluent book, she proves to be a passionate and gifted spokesperson."
—*Publishers Weekly*

For *A Different Kind of Listening*

"A compelling recounting of the rewards and shortcomings of psychoanalysis ... rich with discovery."
—*Kirkus Reviews*

"A moving, provocative, and eminently readable book that raises crucial questions for those concerned with psychoanalysis and self-knowledge."
—Elizabeth Lloyd Mayer, *Journal of the American Psychoanalytic Association*

Everywhere a Guest, Nowhere at Home

A NEW VISION OF ISRAEL AND PALESTINE

KIM CHERNIN

North Atlantic Books
Berkeley, California

Published by
North Atlantic Books
P.O. Box 12327
Berkeley, California 94712

Cover photo by Felix Spira
Cover design © Ayelet Maida, A/M Studios
Book design by Jan Camp
Printed in the United States of America

Everywhere a Guest, Nowhere at Home: A New Vision of Israel and Palestine is sponsored by the Society for the Study of Native Arts and Sciences, a nonprofit educational corporation whose goals are to develop an educational and cross-cultural perspective linking various scientific, social, and artistic fields; to nurture a holistic view of arts, sciences, humanities, and healing; and to publish and distribute literature on the relationship of mind, body, and nature.

North Atlantic Books' publications are available through most bookstores. For further information, visit our Web site at www.northatlanticbooks. com or call 800-733-3000.

Library of Congress Cataloging-in-Publication Data

Chernin, Kim.
  Everywhere a guest, nowhere at home: a new vision of Israel and Palestine / Kim Chernin.
    p. cm.
  Summary: "A collection of passionate and personal essays on the author's struggle to remain proudly Jewish while critiquing Israel's treatment of the Palestinian people"—Provided by publisher.
  ISBN 978-1-55643-820-2
  1. Arab-Israeli conflict—Influence. 2. Military occupation—Social aspects—West Bank. 3. Israel—Ethnic relations. 4. Palestinian Arabs—Civil rights—Israel. 5. Refugees, Palestinian Arab. 6. Jews—Attitudes toward Israel.
7. Reconciliation—Political aspects. 8. Chernin, Kim. I. Title.
  DS119.7.C4654 2009
  956.05—dc22
                                                                      2009007131

1 2 3 4 5 6 7 8 9 VERSA 14 13 12 11 10 09

Even the most basic questions are unanswerable—
mystic, moral or pragmatic. Is the Jewish people at
home here, or in exile; is it loyal or subversive, chosen
or proscribed? The divine was always in dispute with
this people, and always present in it: what a condition,
what a movement! Countless its ways, but the goal in
darkness. Immense its influence on the alien world;
infinite its loneliness.

—Karl Wolfskehl

This book is dedicated to Amira Hass,
most just and courageous of Israeli journalists.

Acknowledgments

Heartfelt thanks to:

Renate Stendhal, as always my first, most inspiriting, and demanding reader;

Tony Rudolf, for his vast knowledge and judicious weighing of every word I wrote;

Erin Wiegand, my thoughtful and insightful editor, who is uniquely responsible for helping this book into the world.

I am deeply grateful for the conversations I've had with Randall Alifano, Ellery Akins, Hathaway Barry, Peter Barnes, Bob Cantor, Cornelia Durrant, Mary Goulart, Carol Jessop, and Leah Lazar.

The essay "A Land without a People" appeared in an earlier form in *Seven Pillars of Jewish Denial* (North Atlantic Books, 2004).

Contents

I

I Think of Israel in the Night

The Jewish people has no fatherland of its own, though many motherlands; it has no rallying point, no centre of gravity, no government of its own, no representatives. It is everywhere a guest, nowhere at home.

—Leo Pinsker, 1882

I was a child when the Jewish homeland was proclaimed in Israel. It was and would always remain eight years younger than I was. From the beginning there was something protective in my feelings for this homeland. I adopted it, my fragile little sister. My parents were hostile to the idea of a Jewish state, especially one immediately at war with its Arab neighbors. They said we Jews had no right to be in Palestine and no need for a homeland of our own. They said we would become a ghetto among the nations. They did not like our Jewish identity if it was used to keep us from recognizing our solidarity with all the working people in the world. I wasn't impressed. My love for the homeland survived all opposition; it is alive in me to this day, but today I know I must overcome it, as well as I can, if I am to write responsibly about Judaism, especially when the focus of this thinking is on the Middle East.

Overcome is probably not the right word. I imagine I will have to reason my way through this old attachment to my homeland. I will have to move delicately around it, keeping a close eye on the way it bends and influences my perceptions. I want to sit here quietly reasoning; or rather, this quiet is the state I wish to achieve through this process of reasoning, as I gather in everything I have learned and been told and all that I have seen for myself about my homeland. Do I still regard Israel as my adopted homeland? I will find out.

Reasoning may also not be the right word, certainly not if it excludes deep feelings, irrationalities, the struggle with uncertainties, the emergence of conflicts and divided loyalties. I would like to think of reasoning as a state of mind that holds all these, cherishes them as it studies them, takes the study of them as its primary task and responsibility. I would like compassion to arise in place of judgment, understanding where partisan opinion has already lived a long enough life. My greatest ambition is to hold two contending points of view simultaneously, without allowing either one to exclude or silence the other. I want to listen to them, place them in dialogue, look at the world through the lens of both, not choosing between them, just listening and taking in. Somewhere, far, far down the road, I glimpse a possibility of reconciliation. Yet, I am reluctant to approach it too easily. I prefer a long and tangled, steep and rugged intellectual path on which many have walked before me and on which I myself have been wandering for many years.

I hope that by now I have come far enough to look back and make sense of what it has been like. All along, the hardest work for me, the child-Zionist, has been the struggle to take in the Palestinian point of view. "Take in" has not meant agree with it, although it has involved questioning some cherished ideas about my people and our land.

I found this tough work, moral, ethical, intellectual, psychological, and spiritual, all at the same time. I passed through recurrent cycles of not caring to know what there was to know. I was always ready with Great Thoughts: the ancient roots of our exiled people, our suffering, the cherished dream that had held us together as a people in exile over thousands of years. These ideas still hold great power for me. But they are ideas I now regard as very dangerous; in their name one can justify just about anything.

No claim that came up from the Palestinian side could enter my consciousness until it forced its way through these barriers, over and again, and then again. When the Palestinian point of view finally arrived, exhausted and threadbare with this struggle to get in, it faced my own exhaustion and was held in suspension before I could take it up and use it for thinking. In this process I am still involved.

I am not implying that our Jewish ways of seeing things are wrong. Only that they made it hard for me to listen to the Palestinians.

I have come to no conclusions, as yet. How could I, with my Jewishness so long present in me and my listening-to-others so newly established?

One discovery I did make: it is not wise to confuse people and their leaders with the extremists among them, or with their representatives or the representations made by themselves or others.

Another discovery: the compassion and sympathy I had always felt for the Jewish people in dispersion, and by extension for exiles, refugees, and impoverished people living under difficult conditions, could now include the Palestinians. Everywhere a guest, nowhere at home: could I deny this description to them?

Six words that tell the story of two peoples.

II

A Land without a People

When I first went to Israel in 1971 I was a naïve but ardent Zionist, intending to spend my life on a kibbutz in the Galilee and to become an Israeli citizen.

What is a naïve Zionist in 1971? Using myself as an example I would say: a naïve Zionist is a person who knows nothing substantive about Zionism as a movement, maybe has never heard of Herzl, certainly knows nothing about the roots of Zionism in the Russian Pale, has never read a word about the Zionist conferences in Switzerland or the Balfour Declaration, and so on. A naïve Zionist, such as I was, hears that there is a Jewish homeland. A place filled with Jews, a country that celebrates Jewish holidays, a homeland where all Jews from all over the world are welcome; a country with a kibbutz system that is a form of socialism and where you can work on the land. I had been wanting to live in that place since I was eight years old.

Back home, before leaving, I argued almost daily with my mother, an extreme left-wing radical, about the Jews' right to a home in our historical, holy, therefore inalienable land. I saw every reason to think of Israel as "ours." It was the land where Hebrew had been born, the land promised to us in our Bible, the Holy Land for which we had yearned for thousands of years. My mother thought people who had lived there more recently had a better claim. I felt that she had no imagination, no sense of epic history, no appreciation for the power of a great dream.

She drove me to the airport; we were still arguing when we pulled up in the passenger zone. This time, because I was leaving, I would have the last word. I had a right to live my own life wherever I chose to live it. And what a hypocrite she was anyway, working her whole life to bring about a socialist system and then not wanting her daughter to live in one.

I slammed the door so hard the car shook.

A naïve Zionist off to spend her life in Israel. But once established on my kibbutz on the Lebanese border, I began to notice things that disrupted my complacency. We used to ride down to our orchards on kibbutz trucks with Arab workers from the neighborhood, who occasionally invited us to visit them in their village. We liked sitting on a rug on a dirt floor, eating food cooked over an open fire, drinking water from the village well. Above all, we loved the kerosene lamps that were lit and set in a half circle around us as it grew dark. It was exotic and it was romantic, and walking home it occurred to me that our kibbutz had running water, electricity, modern stoves. Our neighbors were gracious, generous, and friendly, although I had learned by then that the land the kibbutz occupied had once been theirs or had been land they had worked sometimes for generations for absentee landlords. We Jews had been a people without a land, but the land we came to cultivate and develop had not been a land without a people.

That is what my mother had been trying to tell me.

The path from this troubled awakening to my later ability to be critical of Israel has been long and complex. Over the years I have spoken with other Jews who have traveled this same path, and to many more who haven't. In each of us I have detected the same mental obstacles that made it hard, sometimes impossible, to see what was there before our eyes.

Let us imagine seven pillars that uphold this narrowing of vision in many contemporary Jews.

1. We begin with a conviction that Jews are always in danger, always have been, and therefore are in danger now.

   Which leads to:

2. The insistence that a criticism is an attack and will lead to our destruction.

   Which is rooted in:

3. The supposition that any negativity toward Jews (or Israel) is a sign of anti-Semitism and will (again, inevitably) lead to our destruction.

   Which is enhanced by:

4. Survivor's guilt.

   Which contains within itself:

5. A hidden belief that we can change the past.

   Which hides from us:

6. A disturbing calculus by which we measure violence.

   Which finally brings us to:

7. The conviction that our beliefs, our ideology (or theology), matter more than the lives of other human beings.

Obstacles 1–3: Blindness

The first three obstacles reveal a cluster of convictions about Jewish endangerment which tend to reinforce one another in insidious ways. We can trace the development of this consciousness. It goes something like this: We keep a watchful eye out, we read the signs, we detect innuendo, we summon evidence, we become, as we imagine it, the ever-vigilant guardians of our people's survival. Endangered as we imagine ourselves to be, endangered as we insist we are, any negativity, criticism, or reproach, even from one of our own, takes on exaggerated dimensions—we come to perceive such criticism as a life-threatening attack.

Our proclivity for this perception is itself one of our unrecognized dangers. Bit by bit, as we gather evidence to establish our perilous position in the world, we are brought to a selective perception of that world. With our attention focused on ourselves as the endangered species, it seems to follow that we ourselves can do no harm. We are so busy warding off danger we become unaware that we endanger others. As a people we fill up, we occupy, all the endangerment-space. When other people clamor for a portion, we believe they are trying to deny us our right to this ground. At its most vehement, our sense of ever-impending Jewish peril brings down on us an almost perfect blindness to the endangerment of others and to the role we might play in it.

When I lived in Israel I practiced selective perception. I was elated by our little kibbutz on the Lebanese border until I recognized that we were living on land that had been the home of other people. When I didn't ask how we had come to acquire that land, I practiced blindness.

Long before I went to Israel, how many years before I cannot any longer say, my mother would bring out a rolled-up poster of a Palestinian youth. It may have been sometime in the early seventies. It showed a very young man lying in the road in a pool of his own blood. This image caused a major family breakdown when she showed it to her brother, who stormed out without saying good-bye and didn't speak to her again for years. On another occasion, there was an even more violent scene with the father of an old high school friend of mine. My mother unrolled the poster, and he jumped up from the couch, raised his fist at her, and stormed from the room. Before slamming the door behind him, he shouted back: "This time, Rose, you've gone too far. Next thing, you'll be calling Israeli soldiers. ..." Here he caught himself, but couldn't hold back. "You'll be calling Jewish people who defend their lives. ..." Another break, and then, finally, the unthinkable word: "You'll be calling us *Fascists*."

Slam. My friend and I looked at my mother in shock, amazed to find her silent and unperturbed. Her Palestinian friends felt no taboo against recognizing similarities between the Nazi occupations of Europe and the Israeli occupation of the West Bank and Gaza. Where my mother saw martyrdom, victimization, tragedy in the image of the fallen youth, I saw a dangerous enemy stopped short in his effort to destroy our people. My friend's father, who lived in constant dread of Jewish annihilation, may have seen a necessary vengeance, an image of justice. I don't know what my friend saw. I drove her home in silence and we never met up with one another again. My mother, for her part, never said a word. When I stared at her she merely narrowed her eyes and looked back with an expression that implied: "I will think my own thoughts no matter who objects to them."

The fixed certainty of impending Jewish destruction: wherever we look, we see nothing but its confirmation, the same old story, always about to happen. In the grip of this persuasion, any other possibilities of meaning are swept away; we are unable to imagine things, even for a split second, from another's point of view. It took me years to overcome this blindness. My thoughts would return to the scene in my mother's living room; I would pore over the image, the outrage, the silence.

One day, during an enormous inner struggle, most of what I believed about most of what mattered most to me fell apart. Martin Buber refers to such an event as "an elemental reversal, a crisis and a shock."[1] (I will narrate the background to this crisis as we go along.) Years of images and impressions I had kept at one remove came resoundingly together. I saw what my mother had seen: a boy gunned down by a superior military force; a very young man fighting for the survival of his people, who were far more endangered than ours.

To see a people far more endangered than ours: this is the first step in the dismantling of blindness.

Obstacles 4–5: Survivor's Guilt

I was walking across the beautiful square in Nuremberg a couple of years ago and stopped to read a public sign. It told this story: during the Middle Ages, the town's governing body, wishing to clear space for a square, burned out, burned down, and burned up the Jews who had formerly filled up the space. End of story. After that, I felt very uneasy walking through the square, and I eventually stopped doing it.

I felt endangered, of course, a woman going about through Germany wearing a Star of David. But more than that, I experienced a conspicuous and dreadful self-reproach at being so alive, so happily on vacation, now that I had come to think about the murder of my people hundreds of years before. After reading that plaque I stopped enjoying myself and began to look for other

signs and traces of the mistreatment of Jews. If I had stayed longer
in Nuremberg, if I had gone further in this direction, I might soon
have come to believe that I, personally, and my people, currently,
were threatened by the contemporary Germans eating ice cream
in outdoor cafés in the square.

On another occasion, also in Germany, while visiting the
town hall in a small city near Limburg, I read a notice about the
"ehemalige Jüdische Gemeinschaft." The notice was referring to the
synagogue where the "former Jewish community" had once wor-
shipped. There was a map showing the path to the synagogue
from the town hall. As I followed the path the words followed
me. *"Ehemalige Jüdische Gemeinschaft, ehemalige Jüdische Gemeinschaft."* I felt that I had heard, stated factually, almost casually, and
compressed into three terrifying words, the entire history of the
destruction of my people by the Nazis.

It is not surprising that Germany brings out this sensitivity. I
have dreams of trains. I am watching the train go by; in the next
instant I am looking out from behind bars and someone else is
watching the train pass. Have I managed to exchange my life for
another's? I visit Germany because my partner is German; I am
made welcome in my German family; I am familiar with the language, and I have, since I was an adolescent, defended Germans
against the charge that they had enacted a unique evil, which no
other culture or people could perpetrate. Details change, numbers vary, the dark genius for impeccable organization of mass
murder may not be easily found among another people. But the
commitment to genocide and the ability to carry it out is not
unique to Germans. I visit Germany in spite of the associations it
calls up, and sometimes, I think, because of them. I seem to want
to feel that I am in the midst of the terror, that the persecutions
are happening, that I can escape or perhaps, better yet, still help

others. When I go to Germany I do what I can to enhance this sensibility, although of course I do not admit this to myself. Why enhance it? The subterranean reasoning must go something like this: if we live in a world as dangerous to us as the Holocaust was to our people, we can be that much closer to the victims of the Holocaust, we can know their apprehension and terror; perhaps we may yet succeed in taking their suffering upon ourselves.

There are dark moods; they occur when I think about Israel in the night, when any suffering seems preferable to the nagging, restless guilt that can plague us as survivors. Amos Elon, most thoughtful of Israeli journalists, describes it like this: "The Holocaust was an event many native Israelis felt they had experienced vicariously, as it were, irrespective of age, origin, or education. Even many non-Jewish Israelis, including Arabs and Druze, share in the same feeling by a kind of osmosis."[2]

I try to argue: I was an infant, a small child when the Holocaust occurred. How can I be responsible for what happened? But reasoning does no good; I have cast myself upon my vulnerability, there I must remain. It seems that no victory on the Israeli side, no crushing of the perceived enemy, no destruction of their wells or dismantling of their infrastructure can change our fear that the enemy will rise up to defeat us. Nothing, no act or behavior by our now powerful homeland with the fourth-largest army in the world, can alter this perception of ever-present danger.

We will not let it happen again. But this claim, which seems to point exclusively into the future, is also yoked to our inability to accept the past. By keeping the past alive, by living it all over again, we attempt to alter it. Hidden within the militant "never again" is the anguished cry: "It did not happen. It will never have happened."

Obstacle 6: The Calculus

We Jews are an old people. The past that comes along with us, thousands of years old, fills us with longing for our ancient homeland, for the idea of a homeland, for Jerusalem, for the Temple, and for what these places have meant to our people. We celebrate the fact that these shared memories, enacted in yearly rituals, have held us together in a long exile. We remember our bondage in Egypt and our expulsion from Spain and the forced flight of our people, hunted across continents. We are proud of our descent from King David, we recite his psalms, we read the prophets, we believe (many of us) that we were exiled from the Holy Land because of our sins. But there is a danger here: it is this past, and its suffering, and the scale of its suffering, which create a strange and troubling calculus that does its work just beyond our self-awareness as Jews. When we behave roughly to another people, we judge our behavior by what has been done to us. Is our behavior as bad as that? If not (and since very little is likely to match our two thousand years) we have granted ourselves a frighteningly large range of permissible violence. We have an enormous difficulty imagining Palestinian lives and the suffering involved in them. Are we whispering to ourselves, "But our suffering was much worse. We haven't driven them into concentration camps, smothered them in gas, burned them to cinders. If they have had to leave their homes behind, to live uncomfortably in other parts of the Arab world, how bad is that when placed alongside our thousands of years of persecution and exile?"

If we learn that no Arab state (apart from Jordan) has granted Palestinians citizenship during the last fifty years, our ghettos and exclusions over the last two thousand years rise up to diminish theirs. If our violence is not as bad as what was done to us, do we need to take our violence seriously? Do we even have the ability to conceive of it as violence?

There is a widespread assumption among our people that the vanished victims of the Holocaust would approve of what we do to make sure their fate cannot again befall the Jewish people. Is it fair, however, to assume that their suffering and death would hold no other meaning for them than a recourse to violence and vengeance? How can we assume that they would want their suffering to legitimize anything "not as bad as what happened to them"?

There is another poster. It shows a single Palestinian woman facing a massive Israeli bulldozer. Looking at this image one immediately understands what Primo Levi (a survivor of Auschwitz) meant when he claimed that the Palestinians are the Jews' Jews. He did not have to complete this equation. Silently, it points an accusing finger at the people who are turning the Palestinians into Jews. Can we face the fact that we make use of the Holocaust as a way of diminishing, in our own eyes, the magnitude of our violence against another people?

It is not easy to encounter the idea that we are using the six million, hiding behind them, importing our own meanings into their suffering and death. It took me a long time to face this charge; to recognize that some part of my ever-increasing concern with Holocaust victims, Holocaust books, and first-person Holocaust accounts was serving as a cover-up, distracting my gaze from a living, contemporary struggle in which another people were engaged.

Another step in the dismantling of blindness.

Obstacle 7: Ideology

The Israeli army that defends our homeland fires upon innocent civilians. What justifies the behavior of this army? When the Palestinian suicide bomber blows up a hotel full of Passover celebrants we see clearly that this is an instance of unholy violence. When we attack a refugee camp of impoverished Palestinians in our search for terrorists, this, in our eyes, is a violence purified by our history and our destiny. We are puzzled that much of the world doesn't see our situation in the same way.

Though we rarely dwell on it, the Torah is full of ancient stories marked by tribal violence done in the name of Jehovah. We know the story of Elijah wrangling with the prophets of Baal on Mount Carmel. The prophet wins a clear victory for Jehovah over the Canaanite gods. We know, but don't make much of the fact as we retell the story, that after Elijah won the contest on Jehovah's behalf he took the prophets of Baal down to the brook of Kishon and slew them there. All 450 of them. I have not heard of or read a midrash that elaborates this massacre and warns us against these propensities.

I once wrote an article about the traces of goddess worship in the Torah. When I cited this example of Elijah and the prophets, my three editors, all intelligent and well-educated Jewish women, were uneasily eager to have me supply a footnote for this contentious assertion. They were as surprised as I had once been to find the account of this violence in the Torah itself. And yet they had certainly read Kings II.

In a similar vein: We celebrate the military victories of Joshua. But do we really take in what they involved? "Joshua, and all Israel with him, went on up from Elon to Hebron. They attacked it, took it and struck it with the edge of the sword, with its king, all the places belonging to it and *every living creature in it*" (Joshua 10:37; my italics). I have yet to hear a rabbi help us imagine this event in which women and children, the very young and the very old, are put to the sword by our own Hebrew warriors.

In our return to Israel we have claimed a right to our ancient homeland and a descent from the Hebrews who took possession of the land. We do not seem to have imagined the vital danger of inheriting, along with the land, the early Hebrew propensity toward violence, conquest, displacement of a people who were already there. I can't count the number of times I read the story of Joshua as a tale of our people coming into their rightful possession of their promised land without stopping to say to myself, "But this is a history of rape, plunder, slaughter, invasion, and the destruction of other peoples."

That boy over there with the black face mask and a rock. That is a terrorist. This boy over here with a submachine gun, firing on the boy with the rock, he is a soldier.

A trick of language? I was once persuaded to show up for rifle training when I lived on my kibbutz, although as an American citizen I wasn't required to attend. And whom did I imagine I would shoot? And kill? I, who cannot kill a moth? I never imagined it had to do with killing. Because of the language I used (*I lift this rifle in fulfillment of my pledge to reclaim my homeland*) the training became a pure act, necessary, not even in need of justification.

Shlomo Lavie, a well-known leader of the Israeli Labor Party, the Mapai, declared that the "transfer of Arabs out of the country in my eyes is one of the most just, moral and correct things that can be done."[3]

Another Mapai leader, Avraham Katznelson, felt that nothing was "more moral, from the viewpoint of universal human ethics, than the emptying of the Jewish state of the Arabs and their transfer elsewhere ... This requires ... force."[4]

It may indeed have required force. But moral, ethical, universally sanctioned force? David Ben-Gurion, Israel's first prime minister, shared these sentiments. "We must expel Arabs and take their places ... and if we have to use force ... to guarantee our own right to settle these places—then we have force at our disposal."[5]

Another of our early founders was prepared to go further: "All moral enterprises are carried out through compulsion ... The transfer [of Palestinians] is a just, logical, moral and humane program in all senses."[6]

It is not good enough that some moral enterprises might require compulsion. Now it is all such enterprises, every imaginable moral enterprise that requires force. Nor is it sufficient that under certain conditions the use of force might be justified. Now the expulsion of the Palestinians is the most moral imaginable act "from the viewpoint of universal human ethics." I suppose our early leaders might have been talking themselves into believing these words. But so much the worse if they believed them, and so much the worse for us if we do. We are excited by these grand thoughts; at their urging we fly up onto a higher plane where everything is certain, preordained, lawful, commanded. Suddenly, we are able to disregard the Jewish teachings that a single human life and the saving of it are more important than obeying the laws of the Sabbath. This is a bold and Jewish ethical idea and soundly rebukes our wish to believe in the sanctity of Jewish violence.

Taken together, the examination of these suppositions and convictions, gnawing away at the seven pillars that uphold them, promises to make us uneasy. That is my hope.

Some American Jews will soon set out to join settlements on the West Bank or to volunteer for the Israeli army. Others have gone to Ramallah to help the Palestinians, hoping that their presence there will make it harder for the Israeli army to smash through the city with tanks. Still others have been talking about a peace brigade that will be established along the still undefined and ever-expanding Israeli border, a human buffer zone between the Israelis and the Palestinians.

Here is our Jewish identity, stretched out between these extremes. It's up to us; we are free to choose. Where shall we place ourselves?

III

Where Facts End

A fine mesh, so delicately woven it lets you look but keeps you from seeing what you are determined not to see. I could have gone a lifetime with a veil of not-seeing before my eyes. Stitch by stitch, piece by piece, over many years, it was hard work to get rid of it. I'm not sure if you can fully succeed in dismantling a worldview that has grown up with you, so mixed in with who you've been and who you are. Fortunately, some of the shredding seems to happen of itself; inevitably there are shocks and insights along the way, which manage to set you in conflict with yourself.

This is the story of considerable conflict: of the way a world-view is acquired and then brought down.

Ideology does not have to be taught; it can be achieved seamlessly by coming to share the ideas of the people with whom one lives. Many of the other kibbutz members, the Israelis in particular, had been taught Zionist history since their earliest school days. By the time I returned to America I shared their view of the founding of our homeland, the 1948 war, the refugee problem, and the near-annihilating force of the Arab invasion.

When I try now to reconstruct the process through which I acquired this view of Zionist history I remember anecdotes I told many times in the following years. When I lived in Israel there was no security road along the Israeli-Lebanese border. Our kibbutz, directly on the border with Lebanon, high up in the Galilee, was exposed to shelling from the Lebanese side. There was a reserve unit of soldiers stationed on the kibbutz to stand guard at night and assist the regular army in tracking down infiltrators who were said to have slipped across the border. When we left the kibbutz we had to drive down from the mountain, cross through the valley, and drive up another steep and winding road to visit Safed, a trip we made on Simchat Torah, the holiday of rejoicing with the Torah.

Safed was a town with an unmistakable Arab look to its alleys and winding side streets, stone walls and rock steps, houses with eggshell roofs, thick walls, lattice-brocaded windows. Clearly, it had been an Arab city, a place I imagined would have been difficult to leave, with its stunning view of Mount Meron to the north, its multiple terraces and old streets. I remember feeling happy that "we," the Jews, had acquired this beautiful town when its former inhabitants "had left." At the time, that was enough for me; they had left, we had acquired it. Now I have to wonder: what is the state of mind that accepts conditions of this kind unthinkingly? In retrospect, it reminds me of the way some Germans I have met describe how the "Jews went away," leaving open desirable positions as bank managers and the like. At the time, however, I was only mildly interested in my companion's account of the Arabs fleeing voluntarily as the Israel Defense Forces took over the town. I suppose the word "voluntarily" might have caught my attention. It's a significant and resonant word, with a capacity to impart one of the important Zionist teachings. The Arabs left of their own free will, we did not push them out; they fled in a state of irrational fear, or they were advised by their leaders to abandon their villages and towns. In that moment I came to believe what my companions on the kibbutz believed about the way we Jews acquired Palestine.

On the way back, late at night, we decided to take the short route by driving home along the border. We knew this was dangerous; we could have been shot at by Arabs or by our own soldiers, who were at that time constructing the security road. My companions had heard stories of the way Arabs had massacred Jews during the civil war, and one of them told a story about the Arab massacre of nearly sixty orthodox Jews in Hebron; that had been long before the civil war, during the 1920s, when the Arabs began to be hostile toward their Jewish immigrant neighbors. In this version of events Jews had never attacked their Arab neighbors and never would have if the Arabs hadn't started the civil war or if Israel hadn't been invaded by Arab armies.

We were stopped by an Israeli soldier who sternly told us it was forbidden, by day or night or any other time, to drive the road. He lectured us about the danger we were in from both sides but smiled indulgently when he learned we were from our border kibbutz and radioed ahead so that we would have safe passage.

We came home with a great story to tell, and I with another piece of imparted Zionist teaching. We, on our side, obeyed the purity of arms to which our soldiers were dedicated; the stern and smiling fresh-faced man who had stopped us along the road embodied everything good and decent you could want to believe about an Israeli soldier. They, faceless and ominous across the border with their rifles trained on us, were the aggressors. Our behavior toward them had been necessary in the name of our security.

Of course, these things don't have to be spelled out—who was in danger, who was violent, who the aggressor was; how large the armies had been on either side; why people, soldiers and civilians, behaved the way they did during a war; whether war justifies behavior that would not occur except for war; who is imperiled, who is strong ... this is, of course, the litany of unsettling questions about the birth of Israel and the beginning of the Palestine refugee crisis. By the time I went back to America, without having read a word of or attended a single lecture on Zionist history, I "knew" the story of our nation's Zionist ascent, knew and accepted every telling of the story most Jews at that time told. I had even learned something about the 1947 UN decision to partition Palestine and how we Jews accepted it and the Arabs refused.

We had gone into the shelters during a night of shelling. We were at that time in the triumphant days between the Six-Day War (1967) and the near-disaster of 1973. We had "taken back" the West Bank for security reasons and because it had been ours in biblical times; one of the women sitting next to me in the shelter reflected sadly on how different things could have been if only the Arabs had accepted the UN partition. Our kibbutz was a far-left kibbutz of the Hashomer Hatzair movement, which had always argued for a binational state, with equal rights for Jews and Arabs. My companion in the shelter did not condemn the Arabs out of hand; she blamed their leaders for what had happened, and she could still imagine (not a popular view) a state in which Jews and Arabs lived together. Nevertheless, she was in no doubt that the Yishuv, the Jewish community, had been in terrible danger at the beginning of the civil war, and even more so when the Arab armies invaded. I, who knew nothing about these events, was in no doubt either. Who could be in doubt? Our Israel was surrounded by millions of hostile Arab neighbors who had crossed our border with the intent to drive us into the sea.

The process through which this "education" was brought into question occurred almost as casually as the original education itself. It did not come about through reading and study (not yet); it seemed to arrive almost of itself, to be gathered in, once again, anecdotally. But this process, while seemingly casual, was nevertheless troubled and stormy; it pitted me against myself and everything I wanted to believe about the Jewish people. There were weeks of near-obsession when I could not think of anything else. Back and forth in conversation and argument, within myself, against myself, the doubts and beliefs about what had happened in Palestine before and after 1948 staged a shouting match. I tried many times to get the two sides to sit down at the table and negotiate; I wanted each side to reason and be open to the other side. I wanted to sit quietly and take in what both sides had to say, to place these version of events side by side so that the virtues and weaknesses on both views could be studied. Unfortunately, I was years ahead of myself, trying to do then what I am still trying to do today as I write this account, not yet certain that I can accomplish it.

Some years later, back in Berkeley again, I was listening to two Palestinian women in conversation in a café. They were discussing the fact that both their mothers had been born in Palestine and had left after 1948. I heard the word *"nakba."* The two women leaned toward each other across the table, their heads almost touching. Some of their conversation was lost to me. After a time, I heard the word again and in its new context figured out that it meant something terrible. Something terrible had happened to both their mothers, and here were the daughters in a Berkeley café discussing it. I left the café without giving their conversation much thought, but I took away a new word and with it an opening into a very different point of view than I had before encountered. The new point of view was in the word itself, in the way the two women had leaned toward each other to speak it, in the fact that we were at adjacent tables in my regular café, where I had seen them before, had thought of them admiringly as two good friends and seen them as women like myself and not as Palestinians.

Nakba. Nakba. Nakba.

At that time I had a friend, a professor of political science, who had critical thoughts about Israel. Some weeks later, when I was having coffee with him, I asked him about the word. He knew it; he'd known it for some time but had hesitated, with good reason, to mention it to me. Back then I wasn't known for my calm and rational style of discourse; when facing disagreement, especially about Israel, I often flew into a rage, raised my voice, interrupted my friend, trying as hard as I could to drown him out while trying as hard as I could not to. I had been known, on some occasions, to push back my chair and storm out of the café resolving to end the friendship or at least never to speak with that particular person about anything serious again. This time I listened.

Nakba meant "catastrophe." It was the way Palestinians referred to what had happened to them in 1948.

It is easy enough to forget a foreign word, not so easy to quell the apprehension it stirs up. I certainly forgot the word many times, while the history it carried, the version of events it held, the implications it brought, the difficult challenges it presented, seemed to be drawn to me and gathered in, magnetically. The faceless enemy, the dark threat from the other side of the border, had acquired a face and therefore could no longer be considered simply an enemy. There was another people there, people who had mothers and stories and homes and villages and orchards and families, each with their own unique sense of disaster. Voluntarily or not, they were people who had lost a homeland as we had acquired ours. What if they had fled in fear expecting to come home again? What if they hadn't fled voluntarily? What if they'd been driven out?

A struggle of this kind, set going within the self, will occasion sleepless nights. Once it starts up it will rage on for years. For every argument a counterargument, for every point of view another way to look at things, for every accusation a justification, for every assertion a counterclaim. Facts? Establish the facts? I was trying to place the Palestinian version of events against the Zionist account of them, the old Zionist account against the work of more recent historians. I was fighting within myself to figure out what really happened, what happened first, what happened next—or who did what to whom and for what reason.

At times the obsession with Israel would die down. Months, sometimes a year or two would pass before, inevitably, it showed up again.

I had returned from Israel in 1972. I was still engaged in this debate during the 1980s and well into the 1990s. I remember a violent argument that broke out on New Year's Eve, as my preoccupation with Israel crossed over into the twenty-first century.

The more I learned the more uncertain I became about the present. Whom was I to believe? The Palestinians did not agree with one another. Some called for armed struggle and the liberation of Palestine; others encouraged the peace accords; some saw the peace accords as a stalling effort on the part of Israel as it continued to build settlements in occupied territory.

Israelis did not agree with one another, either. We Jews were old-style Zionists who believed in the Zionist version of events, or we were revisionist historians who rewrote the history of 1948. We were members of religious movements that believed God had promised us the land and therefore justified our violence against anyone who questioned our possession of it. Or we were men and women who had seen at first hand and with horror what had happened to the Palestinian population. "We came, shot, burned, blew up, repelled, pushed, and exiled. What the hell are we doing here?" demands the Israeli novelist S. Yizhar.[7]

Everyone agreed that a flight had taken place in 1948, but how many Palestinians had been involved, and why they had fled, remained contentious. Zionists claimed that the Palestinian refugees from 1948 represented a "population exchange" with the Jews who left the Arab world in the 1950s. Palestinian historians regarded this claim as "mendacious and misleading."[8] Was it fair to compare the flight of Palestinians in 1948 with the voluntary exodus of Jews from hostile Arab nations? And how voluntary were these mass departures? Readers must take up the issue and resolve it, or not, for themselves.

This is the place where facts end. Zionist claim: 850,000 Sephardic Jews left Arab states to come to Israel. Palestinian claim: It was 600,000 Sephardic Jews. Zionist claim: 600,000 Palestinians left Israel during the troubles of 1948. Palestinian claim: It was 850,000 Palestinians. There was, depending on your numbers, an equal exchange of populations from Arab states to Israel, from Israel to Arab states. Or, depending on your numbers and your interpretation of them, there was not.

In talking about hundreds of thousands of people, does it matter if there is a disproportion in how many on either side have been unsettled by war and hostility? Perhaps it does matter; but in what way?

Point: There were more Jews in Palestine than Arabs at the time of the partition. *Counterpoint:* The Arabs far outnumbered the Jews.

Assertion: The Arabs were not dispossessed of their land; the land they worked belonged to absentee landlords who had always exploited them. *Denial:* The Palestinians had worked the same land for generations, tended the same orchards, lived in the same villages; the land was theirs even if they did not own it.

Claim: The Jews descended from the ancient Hebrews and therefore had the prior claim to the land. *Counterclaim:* It was the Palestinians who descended from the indigenous Canaanites.[9]

Appeal to memory: We Jews have always longed for Eretz Yisroel as our ancient homeland. Witness our liturgy. *Refutation:* The Jewish preoccupation with Palestine began with Zionism in the nineteenth century.

The Palestinians claimed the Jews were an occupying, colonial power, which could and would some day be driven out; we Jews, always part of this land, had nowhere else to go. We Jews knew we had behaved righteously in securing our homeland; the Palestinians knew they had been violently and illegally disposed of theirs. They knew they were the victims of our violent occupation; we knew at any moment we might be blown up and victimized by them.

The idea that I could find out what "really happened" became increasingly questionable, then doubtful, and finally absurd. My reading was an education in the infinite regress of reality from the facts assigned to represent it. A "fact" was nothing more than an assertion in an argument; it was used to establish rights, which presumably rested on principles upheld by international law, which might be suspended because of a people's history of suffering, which on the other hand might be irrelevant given that same people's subsequent exercise of violence. Inevitably, the question of rights disappeared into the realities of power, given that power and not rights would determine outcomes. Yet, both sides talked insistently about their rights.[10]

If a people's need was great enough and desperate enough,

need began to confer a right. The Holocaust, as Hitler's attempts to exterminate the Jews later became known, and the refusal of other nations to receive the Jewish refugees, gave us a claim to the land of Israel. The Palestinians derived their rights from the plain fact that they were already there.

What a mess: Rights are an agreement between people. They might be granted by those in power to those who had less power. They might be struggled for and won by a show of force from the powerless. Or people could sit down together and agree to assign rights and respect them. This human arrangement, however, once agreed upon, tended to acquire a self-evident and therefore inalienable quality and to get confused with the type of rights ordained by a higher power or derived from a natural law.

Jefferson's formulation for the American Declaration of Independence: "We hold these truths to be self-evident, that all men are created equal, that they are endowed by their Creator with certain unalienable Rights ..." This famous phrase, derived from John Locke, was intended by Locke as a description of human arrangements, defining the rights (life, liberty, and property) a government should grant to its people. In Jefferson's formulation the government (human) has become the Creator (divine), and the rights that *should* be granted have become self-evident and inalienable.

Watch this confusion at work: Jewish settlers claimed the rights to land in the West Bank and Gaza (Judea and Samaria) because their God had given it to them. Palestinians claimed the rights to this land because they had lived on it, cultivated it, established communities, evolved a culture and a way of life. Where could these two claims, based on entirely different ideas about rights, possibly meet? Hamas's charter calls for the destruction of Israel, with the declared intention to replace the Jewish state with a Palestinian Islamic state. Although Hamas claims that its struggle with Israel is political, the suicide bombers who offer themselves as martyrs hold it to be a self-evident truth that their religion sanctifies their attacks on Israeli civilians. When Israel retaliates, it claims the purely human right to self-defense.

I (which I?) suddenly realized that I no longer knew why I had taken for granted that we Jews had rights to settle in Palestine. I was not an Orthodox Jew; I had certainly not been inspired by religious ideas. Nevertheless, ideas with a religious leaning now cropped up to oppose the other I who argued for the rights of the Palestinian people to the land where they had been living until we Jews came along and forced them out.

A wariness creeps in, a suspicion about that side of the self vigorously marshaling its new arguments. A preparation against thoughts you had no idea you'd ever entertained and couldn't anticipate until they faced you. As if you'd always known they were there and had been struggling with them for a long time. An urgency to know the truth, to determine the facts, some facts, at least one unquestionable fact the contending sides could agree upon.

Good idea, divide your notebook into two sections. Meticulously plotted point and counterpoint in different colored pens. You've run out? You can't think of another defense, another argument, no better strategic sally? Go ahead then, start shouting your head off. Give way to insults, defamations of character, abusive talk. But this is yourself you are calling coward, terrorist, hypocrite, infiltrator, liar. This is not a civil war, a fight between armed belligerents. This is yourself.

No wonder people don't question what they've come to believe.

In Stefan Zweig's chess story, *The Royal Game,* a man has been incarcerated by the Nazis. Apart from times when he is taken for interrogation, he is kept isolated in a spare hotel room, with only a chair, a washstand, and a table. He stares endlessly at the repetitive pattern of the wallpaper. Hour after hour, day after day, the weeks passing, he exchanges no word with anyone, not with the guard who brings him his meals—only with his interrogators. He is an intellectual, and this is the psychological torture the Gestapo has successfully devised for breaking intellectuals to get the information they want. One day, close to a breaking point, the man notices in the waiting room, before his interrogation, a bulge in the pocket of a greatcoat. He manages to slip out a small book and hide it beneath his belt. Back in his room, he is disappointed to find a chess anthology, a collection of 150 championship games. Nevertheless, he works his way through the games until he can play every game in the book from memory. He begins to understand the refinements, the tricks and feints in attack and defense; he grasps the technique of thinking ahead, of planning combinations and riposting ... but now he is bored. The magic has gone out of the game; he has learned everything from both sides. Therefore, he will have to invent new games. But this is chess; he has to play against himself. He knows perfectly well that the attraction of chess lies in the fact that its strategy develops in different ways in two different brains. "If one person tries to be both Black and White you have the preposterous situation that one and the same brain at once knows something and yet does not know it; that, functioning as White's partner, it can instantly obey a command to forget what, a moment earlier as Black's partner, it desired and plotted."[11]

The tension of this impossible self-division becomes more acute. Zweig describes it like this: "No sooner had Ego White made a move than Ego Black feverishly plunged a piece forward;

scarcely had a game ended but I challenged myself to another, for each time, of course, one of my chess-egos was beaten by the other and demanded satisfaction."

This chess man reminded me of myself. In my effort to bring the two sides of the debate closer together I had established within myself each position with its own point of view. Men who crossed into Israel to harvest their orchards were displaced persons longing to return. Men who crossed into Israel were infiltrators, intent on the destruction of the state. There were accusations of massacres, rapes, murder, shootings. The more I read the more abstract they became. They were empty words waiting to be inhabited by meaning. They were there only to do the work of asserting or denying a point in the debate. The humanity in these accounts had receded.

A Palestinian lawyer: "For a moment we revel in our power, the sudden reversal of our fate, our sudden, all too sudden, victory over our enemy. Then we see the old woman crying. It is no longer abstract and faceless victims, it is now harm inflicted on an individual with whom we can identify. She can be our mother, older sister, or neighbor. This changes everything."[12]

The image that changes everything: I could no longer create it.

As a reader, I became uncertain whom the narrator represented: himself, his movement, his school of thought, his people? For whom was he writing? When the narrators said "the Palestinian people" or "the Jewish people," did they mean the leaders, the theorists, the extremists, or the people themselves, who surely did not in all cases agree with their leaders?

I was troubled by how easily one author, referring to the work of another, can misrepresent another's point of view. David Hirst, in *The Gun and the Olive Branch,* claimed that Benny Morris had "made clear that the Jewish community had never been in danger of annihilation on the eve of the 1948 war, and that the Arab armies, poorly trained and equipped ... stood virtually no chance of defeating the new-born state."

In my reading of this book, I had come across very different words:

> Throughout, when examining what happened, the reader must also recall ... the intention of the Palestinian leadership and irregulars and, later, of most of the Arab states' leaders and armies in launching the hostilities in ... invading Palestine in May 1948, to destroy the Jewish state and, possibly, the Yishuv [the Jewish community in Palestine] itself; the fears of the Yishuv that the Palestinians and the Arab states, if given the chance, intended to re-enact a Middle Eastern version of the Holocaust; and the extremely small dimensions, geographical and numerical, of the Yishuv (pop. 650,000) in comparison with the Palestinian Arabs (1.25 million).

Morris made clear that by July of 1948 the leaders of the Yishuv were aware that Israel had won its war for survival. But this statement in no way undermined his earlier assertion (in the same paragraph) that the Yishuv, its people and its leaders, were alarmed. Some pages later, Morris returned unequivocally to this earlier idea: "The war between Israel and the Arab states was protracted and bloody (about 4,000 of the Yishuv's 6,000 dead were killed after 14 May) and the Yishuv's leaders recognized that they faced a mortal threat."

I saw Jews as a persecuted people who had fled to Palestine from the impossibility of living in the Russian Pale. The first immigrants had arrived in 1881 after the assassination of Czar Alexander II and the pogroms that followed, in which hundreds of Jewish communities were attacked by mobs, hundreds of people were killed, and Jewish women were raped by their attackers. How could it be claimed (as it was, by Palestinian historians and by myself arguing against myself) that these people represented a colonial occupation? They came in small groups, bought land, founded settlements and colonies that often failed. They did not exploit the indigenous population in order to prosper; they too struggled for survival. According to one historian, "Agricultural output of the Arab sector rose by 50 percent between 1922 and 1938. Citrus production in the Arab sector grew from 22,000 dunams in 1922 to 144,000 dunams in 1937, roughly the same expansion as in the Jewish sector."[13]

Why "occupation"? Why "colonialism"? Because the Balfour Declaration had been issued by a colonial power? Because the British took the side of the Jews? But wasn't it clear that the English in Palestine during the Mandate period sometimes sided with the Jews, sometimes with the Arabs? The Jews had not been a nation or a state, they'd been a dispersed and scattered people; if you wanted to rise against them and kick them out, to what motherland would they return as citizens?

The debate is restless, evasive, unsettling. Palestinian historians argue that the type of settlements created by Israeli settlers corresponded in their basic structure to settlements created by colonial powers. There were "pure settlement colonies" and "ethnic plantation colonies," and there were attempts to claim all jobs in the land for Jewish laborers, who as a result became ardent nationalists hoping to establish a purely Jewish society.

I am impressed, I shift sides—but only for a moment. A group of Girl Scouts who bought land in the Mojave Desert, built settlements, worked the land themselves or hired people to work it for them, even when they restricted their colonies to other members of the Girl Scouts, would not for any of those reasons become colonialists. The similar forms could not by themselves reproduce the power relations of a colonial nation to the indigenous people it exploited. The making of an exclusivist colony does not of itself make a colonialist.

Members of the Jewish underground, fighting against the British before the State of Israel had been declared, knew the British as a colonial force intent on crushing Jewish resistance. In her memoir, Geula Cohen, a young member of the Stern Gang, refutes the claim that the colonial British consistently took the side of the Jews:

> Adam's latest letter had been impatiently awaited, for one of the events that had taken place since his last communication was the Black Saturday of June 29, 1946. On that day the British had launched a general attack on the Jewish settlement in the hope of breaking the back of the Insurrectionary Front. A curfew was declared in all the major cities and house-to-house searches and confiscations of arms were carried out in dozens of rural co-operatives. The Jewish Agency building in Jerusalem was occupied by troops and the Agency's officials were placed under arrest. Mass arrests took place throughout the country, many of them accompanied by bloodshed.[14]

This is not an easy world to inhabit. I understood why many readers were inclined to stick to the narrative of their side, without struggling to line up the arguments or move flexibly when reasoning from side to side. I certainly was not capable of this grace. Whenever the fuss died down the dispute about colonialism left me sympathetic to the Zionist narrative. I tried, I tried again; I could not break away from this loyalty to my own side. What was the point of borrowing for Jewish-Arab relations a name that defined the behavior of powerful nations toward an exploited, indigenous people? I hated this argument. I hated this debate. No matter how many times I hurled myself back to the Palestinian side, the Jew in me always had the last word. I was far too biased to have the right to an opinion.[15]

Did I believe that since 1967 Palestinian "leaders [had] been jailed and deported by the Israeli occupation regime"? Yes, I did. That "small businesses and farms [had been] made unviable by confiscation and sheer destruction, students prevented from studying, universities closed"? I knew that. And I knew too that "in the mid-1980s Palestinian universities on the West Bank were closed for four years" and that no "Palestinian farmer or business [could] export to any Arab country directly" and that taxes were paid to Israel, collected by Yasir Arafat and his Palestinian Authority but delivered to Israel.[16] But I could not, or I would not, stand for any association of the Jewish homeland with colonialism. Because it made us, an abused and persecuted people, far more powerful than we had been? Because it erased our struggle for survival? Because it was a war over words conducted by people who did not engage in the struggle on the ground, to make up for their failure to be engaged? This charge could not be brought against the PLO in its effort to emulate the Algerians in evicting French settlers. But it was, inevitably, a charge I could bring against myself, against Palestinian and Israeli historians and intellectuals and all readers of books and anyone who tried to reason and think. Now the two sides got going with equal force in an effort to shame each other, cast aspersions, pronounce suspicions, back and forth, each side attacked and attacking, as the argument retreated further from relevance.

And then suddenly it would become relevant again. I recalled Israeli historians who, after the occupation of the West Bank and Gaza in 1967, had used the word "colonialism" to describe their country's relationship to the Palestinians. At first, this seemed a concession to the long-standing Palestinian charge, and I fought against it. But then this idea would edge its way toward a possibility even more disturbing. Colonialism, for all its evils, has had to hold its colonized people in sufficiently tolerable conditions to be able to exploit hem. But was that what was happening in the territories? Did we even have a word to characterize the behavior of a conquering power that wants to rid itself of a conquered people without either transferring or openly destroying them—by making their lives so intolerable they will be driven out? Or, shouts another voice of the inner debate that has detected a treacherous paradox, be forced against their will to choose to leave?

Perhaps it would prove impossible to hold within oneself these embattled points of view without falling into the dilemma of the chess player playing against himself. "The lust to win, to victory over myself increased to a sort of rage; I trembled with impatience, for the one chess-ego in me was always too slow for the other. One would whip the other forward and, absurd as this may seem ... I would call angrily, 'Quicker, Quicker!' or 'Go on, go on!' when the one self in me failed to riposte to the other's thrust quickly enough."

Once released, the chess player in Zweig's story receives a severe warning from his doctor that he must never again succumb to the temptation of chess. I have received no such warning about my struggles, but I have come to the conclusion that no lasting conclusion will be possible for me. I will stay open, unresolved, and uncertain—as long as this is possible for a hothead like me.

IV

Nes Gadol Haya Sham

Nes Gadol Haya Sham. A Great Miracle Happened There. The words we repeat when we play dreidel on Chanukah. Each player spins the top; depending on how it falls we get one nut or all the nuts or half of them, or we have to put some back into the pile. Some say this game was invented to teach Jewish children the Hebrew alphabet when learning Hebrew was forbidden by the Romans. Whoever has collected the most nuts by the end of the game is free to squirrel them away or share them with the other players. My learning of the Hebrew and Yiddish alphabet began with the dreidel.

Nes Gadol Haya Sham. Familiar and beloved words.

One day the words underwent a spontaneous, shocking transformation. *Nakba Gadol Haya Sham.* A Great Catastrophe Happened There. Could one say such a thing? I had never heard it before. Would grammar allow this intermixing of languages, this unexpected verbal miscegenation between Hebrew and Arabic?

I wasn't pursuing my studies at the time; I'd put them aside as too unsettling. Yet here suddenly two incompatible ideas from two radically opposed people were yoked together, a ferocious wordplay, a gift from the unconscious.

What is the space between a catastrophe and a miracle? In this case it spans more than two thousand years between us and the revolt of the Maccabees in 175 BC. A revolt by an indigenous people against the Greek-Seleucid dynasty that was depriving them of self-rule. The space shrinks. Is it in similar terms that the Palestinians view their struggle against Israel? To the Seleucids the Jews must have seemed a stiff-necked, stubborn people from an inferior civilization who would not settle down and let themselves be governed. I've heard more than a few Israeli voices speak of the Palestinians in similar and far more derogatory terms.

An analogy presents itself through a slip of the tongue. How far can this analogy be taken? Judah and his brothers, avoiding direct encounters with the Seleucid army, became guerrilla fighters. Did Antiochus IV Epiphanes, the Seleucid ruler, think of them the way we think of armed Palestinian fighters?

I do not like these thoughts. I'd rather not think them; I am pushing them away almost as fast as they press in. Judah Maccabee is without question a great Jewish hero. In honor of him and his brothers we celebrate Chanukah with its miracle of light. He is ours, he fought in our name, he defeated a superior armed force that kept us from living according to our traditions. Is it such a stretch to imagine the Palestinian people might feel the same way about their struggle and their heroes?

Yes, it is a big stretch, an enormous stretch. It has been driving me to see things as another people might see them, and this is not comfortable. Perhaps the mistake I've been making all along has been my effort to determine a simple truth, a single truth, a set of facts that stays settled no matter who looks at them. A Palestinian village has been destroyed. Is it the same event if it happened as a hazard of war in protection of a young homeland? Or a vastly different event if it was done with the intention to eliminate an indigenous people from their native land? Is there a way to find some middle ground, to listen to both sides without coming to a conclusion about who is right? But here I encounter an ethical problem. The suffering of my own people is widely acknowledged; it has gained a worldwide recognition, while the suffering of the Palestinians has been neglected for decades. In an effort to be fair I would have to raise up what has gone missing to give it adequate representation. What exactly has gone missing? A reviewer in the *New York Review of Books,* writing in 1974, twenty-five years after the State of Israel had been declared, twenty-five years after the Palestinian refugee problem had been created, described his visit to the Israeli Knesset. He was "amazed to hear the members of parliament discuss the question of whether or not the Palestinian problem existed." When he challenged Shulamit Aloni about this, a government minister elected on a civil rights platform, she told him what a great step forward it was for the Knesset simply to be debating the Palestinian problem. A debate of this kind had not been held since the time of Ben-Gurion. "It seemed to me ridiculous that it took Israelis twenty-five years and four wars to recognize the existence of a Palestinian problem. But then it took twenty-five years and four wars for the Arabs to come around to recognizing the existence of the State of Israel. Were I an Israeli, Arab deliberations over recognizing Israel would no doubt have seemed equally absurd."[17]

Equally absurd but not exactly the same. The recognition of a state implies a recognition of its legitimacy. The recognition of a people simply acknowledges that it exists. If I were a Palestinian I would not have been happy about a young woman going to live on a kibbutz in 1971 with no awareness that there was a Palestinian people, or a problem.

Nes Gadol Haya Sham. Nakba Gadol Haya Sham.

A Chanukah celebration in 1982. Israel had just invaded Lebanon in a war of choice. I was spinning the dreidel with a group of kids, explaining to them the meaning of Chanukah and the

Hebrew letters on the dreidel. I had to keep a close eye on myself. I didn't want any slips of the tongue to interfere with my lesson. But on the other hand, why not? Was it too early to let these children know that another people was fighting for its liberation the way our people had fought? To tell them that this other people saw their protest as a liberation struggle and that their struggle was against us?

Wasn't Chanukah the perfect time to introduce this lesson? Plates of latkes were arriving from the kitchen, one of the younger kids wanted to light all the candles on the menorah, our hostess was telling about the miracle of lamps that had burned without oil for eight days and nights during the Maccabees' struggle. This was a celebration, and I was still uneasy with my own thoughts. I had trouble staying present in our gathering; I was searching for a way to think and speak and write about these things without judgment, from a sense of compassion equally deserved by both peoples. When I achieved this there would be time enough to share my thoughts.

V

Thinking the Unthinkable

When I woke up this morning I decided to face everything I had not wanted to face, to know what I had refused to know, and to see clearly what I had not wanted to see.

I did not know what these things were, although I felt their presence; I had no idea how to go about doing what I intended to do. Still, I felt that the intention itself carried weight and would guide me. I got up early and went for a swim, floating on my back and inviting the unthinkable to come visit me. Truly, an odd state of mind, trying to know what you'd rather not know.

While I was getting dressed it occurred to me that if I worked backward from all the times I'd lost my temper during an argument, or provoked an argument and stormed about, there was a good chance I'd find what I was looking for.

What had I argued about last? But obviously there was no last. It had been one long argument over the years, mostly with myself.

I went home and started gathering up my books on Zionism, Palestine, Israel, the Middle East. They were numerous; they had spread out into different rooms. I put them in piles on the floor and sat down with them. This was the right approach. The books were extensively marked with brackets, underlining, marginalia; in many I had written page numbers with cryptic descriptions of what I thought was important. I even had categories called "unthinkable thoughts." Apparently, having marked them unthinkable I promptly went back to not thinking about them. This time it would be different.

I concentrated on finding the unthinkable thoughts that had been written by Jewish writers.

Dov Yermiya writes about his time as a security coordinator of the Ga'aton Regional Council in the Western Galilee, a lieutenant colonel in the IDF. When he has been called up for reserve duty at the beginning of the invasion of Lebanon, in 1982, his wife says to him: "Why are you so excited to be with those murderers? You smell a war and you already rush out to be there? Why didn't you refuse to go? Why don't you all refuse to participate in this murder?"[18]

The murderers she is referring to are in the Israeli army.

His answer is equally shocking. "This time too I will be able to help relieve the suffering, just a little, and will be able to influence some of our soldiers and officers to be human beings, or at least a little less like animals."

What did I make of this when I first read it? In Israel, attitudes toward the army had obviously changed since 1971 when I'd lived on my border kibbutz, where we had been proud of our soldiers. Had the Israeli army changed?

I shuffled through the pages. I had assiduously marked the same type of harsh comments. The commander of his unit, responsible for aid to civilians, orders him to arrange the supply of water to "50,000 people who are concentrated near the nunnery on the sea front, including day-old babies, elderly people, and handicapped people from the city and Ein El-Hilwe refugee camp." It turns out that the people responsible for planning "this huge military operation" have given no thought to such a possibility, "and did not prepare water and food for so many prisoners and for so large a population, part of which lost its homes and all of its property."

I took note of the fact that this unit was there to aid the civilians; they were not at war, they were there to attend the civilian casualties of war.

Dov Yermiya passes the square where the prisoners are concentrated. A young, bearded officer jumps out of a half-track and runs toward him. "Dov, you've got to do something for all these people. Look at how miserable they are; sitting here from morning to evening, starving for bread and dying of thirst. How can you people in the Administration allow this to happen? How did we allow ourselves to become such a cruel army?"

The IDF had become a cruel army? Given the authority of the speakers I could not doubt this: they were Israeli soldiers; they were there at the time. Moreover, I had read this book before. Here, without doubt, were my characteristic marks, but I couldn't believe I had ever made them. The whole story seemed unfamiliar to me. I must have read with relief the comment: "It seems that there are many in the IDF who care, and who are suffering from the fact that we have become a nation of wild warriors, of fire, death, and destruction, as if it was our second nature."

Would it have been possible to take in only the first part of the sentence and to have dismissed the rest? There are many in the IDF who care ...

An old friend of Dov's, a member of Kibbutz Gat, describes the release of Palestinian prisoners and their exhausted, stumbling walk. Another friend says to him: "This was a picture that reminded me of the death march of the Jews in Auschwitz. *Oi vavoi, what have we come to.*"

What have we come to? What had I come to if I could read these words and then forget them? True, they held a most forbidden thought, a half thought, an almost thought. Wasn't he saying that our Israeli soldiers behaved toward the Arabs the way the Fascists had behaved toward us?

Following my marked pages I was carried deep into a story of cruelty: "The prisoners are ordered to sit with their backs bent forward and their heads between their knees. The air is filled with the stink of piss and shit. Not all of them get permission to get up in order to go to the outhouses. Some of the prisoners are sitting there in a state of shock, as if they were unconscious; some are choking and crying silently, out of pain and fear ... Others are sitting in courageous silence staring bravely, directly into my eyes, and I sense the hatred in their look."

There is worse. The testament from a Palestinian prisoner. "From the moment that we were arrested, the beatings began. We were generally beaten with clubs on the head and back while we sat on the ground, our heads forward between our legs, our hands bound behind our backs and our eyes blindfolded with rags. We were beaten without reason or explanation. When we boarded the bus in order to be taken to Israel, the beatings continued ... In the bus, we had to place our heads on the seat in front of us, and every movement or raising of a head was followed by blows."

Dov Yermiya remembers how, at the end of World War II, the Allied soldiers led tens of thousands of German prisoners to camps in the south of Germany. "The orders were clear and precise. 'No one should hurt either the body or the honor of a prisoner.'" Israeli soldiers have told him that their commanders order them to behave toward their prisoners with brutality.

Of course, there were points of relief in the story, and I must have held on to them. Although the Israeli mass media claims that the whole country is behind their leaders, when Dov leaves the front and attempts to collect clothes and supplies for the refugees, he meets with an abundant generosity and concern, especially from members of the kibbutzim. My old kibbutz, so close to the border, is mentioned among one or two others.

A friend of his from Kibbutz Hanita pours out his heart: "Believe me Dov, if I had known that this is what our country would be like, I would have left it thirty years ago." Kibbutz Hanita is not far from the kibbutz where I lived. If this man, an Israeli, is able to think thoughts of this kind, I should also have been able to think them.

Yermiya's condemnation is clear and uncompromising. "The Jewish, Israeli soldier, whose hypocritical commanders and politicians call him the most humane soldier in the world, the IDF which claims to preserve the 'purity of arms' (a sick and deceitful term) is changing its image. For this is what I ran into every step of the way: despicable actions of humiliation, of striking at women and children who wander, confused and miserable, along the sidelines of the war and its aftermath, not knowing their own souls in their fright, hunger and thirst."

There is no need to mention Auschwitz again. Although, a page or two later: "Mahmoud Rahayim of Nazareth is looking for his sisters and relatives. This is how the Jews searched for their relatives after the Holocaust."

The power of wishing not to know must be tremendous. It might be one of the most powerful forces in the world. I keep thinking of little children and how they, when they don't want to be seen, cover up their eyes. Or, if they are afraid of a dog and the dog is running toward them, they shake their head and say: "No dog." This denial is happening in me now. I read and shake my head no. I read on and keep shaking my head. But the mental situation I am studying in poring over my books is worse than denial and more effective. It is a complete and total annihilation of memory. An erasure, as if I had bulldozed over any traces of what I had read. If I did not have my markings and marginalia I would simply not believe that I had ever encountered this text.

Israeli writer Danny Rubinstein, in an op-ed in *Davar,* the Hebrew language daily newspaper: "When you read a diary like this, you want to scream, knock your head against the wall, or just cry, and I'm not exaggerating; it's really terrible. It is not the war which is so horrible in Dov Yermiya's diary, but rather the face of the new Israeli that is unveiled before our eyes."[19]

Yes, yes, one wants to scream. Scream or cry or knock your head against the wall. But I am still reluctant to take in this "face of the new Israeli." Everything in me rebels against it, refuses to receive it. Rubinstein writes: "This is the same Israel who is creating a system of apartheid in the West Bank and the Gaza Strip, who is brutally and proudly trampling on moral values and the dignity of man, it is the animalization and 'rhinocerization' of man."

I suspect few American newspapers would be willing to print this review. But I have read it before, I must have: here it is in the book lying on my lap. I circled it and wrote: "Oh no."

Read, marked, underlined, dog-eared, and not remembered. Is it possible? So it seems.

The same story, in book after book, by Israeli and Palestinian writers. Here is a book about 1948. "All the Israelis who witnessed these events agreed that the exodus, under a hot July sun, was an extended episode of suffering, especially for the Lydda refugees. Some were stripped by soldiers of their valuables as they left town or at checkpoints along the way." Eyewitness: "A multitude of inhabitants walked one after another. Women walked burdened with packages and sacks on their heads. Mothers dragged children after them. ..."[20]

A Palestinian historian: "Of the 418 depopulated villages, 293 (70 per cent) were totally destroyed, and 90 (22 per cent) were largely destroyed. Seven survived, including 'Ayn Karim (west of Jerusalem), but were taken by Israeli settlers. While an observant traveler can still see some evidence of these villages, in the main all that is left is a scattering of stones and rubble."[21]

I was certain I had come across a different number. I went thumbing through my books to find it. Yes, there. Edward Said claiming that Israel "took over what was historical or Mandatory Palestine (destroying and depopulating 531 Arab villages in the process)."[22]

Now I am beginning to see how this works, this half noticing, this ability not to take in. Massacres had been committed in Palestinian villages during the war, and rapes and the shooting of children lined up against a wall. I had read this and had kept wondering, how many children? How many, exactly? How many villages, how many exactly? Not being able to ascertain the exact number must have permitted me to dismiss these troubling facts, arguing that facts could not be relied upon. What did I think when I read that the villages were cleared of people? Did I imagine soldiers of the IDF standing politely next to buses to welcome the soon-to-be refugees aboard? Did I think they took them to some comfortable place on the other side of the border, where good warm food and beds had been prepared? I had been reading to fortify my arguments, to gather points in the never-ending debate. With the focus so narrow, it had been possible to ignore what I didn't want to let in. Yes, yes, these dreadful things are happening, but I am concerned to count how many people and villages and soldiers and children have been involved.

I remember, I clearly remember how in the time of that reading I spoke endlessly about the way stories do not capture the truth of what occurred; I held forth vehemently about the inconsistencies between stories and within any given story. Clearly this preoccupation kept me from knowing what had happened behind the story, where the story was being made.

How convenient!

But here I am now, sitting on the floor with my books, reading them, writing down what I am reading, and still somehow not taking it in. This information is being refused, and I see how. I am getting caught up in the question of whether this clearance of Palestinians from their native villages should be called "transference" or "ethnic cleansing." I have even discovered what seems to me an important distinction. When the Zionists talked (privately) and wrote (in their diaries) about transference, they always included the idea of recompense, of providing sufficient money to make good what had been lost and to help in the resettlement. I had marked many quotes to this end and I was probably right, something different from massacre had been planned. But look at the way this thought can lead to further distinctions, to a continuum that runs from resettlement, through transference, to ethnic cleansing, to genocide. And now I can fuss and debate whether a particular act in a particular village belonged in one or another of these categories. Here too the issue of war enters in, and whether acts that are committed in war, which would not be justified at any other time, are justified. The discussion of that can keep you involved for decades!

But I also marked this, from Ilan Pappé, an Israeli historian, about his own research: "This book is written with the deep conviction that the ethnic cleansing of Palestine must become rooted in our memory and consciousness as a crime against humanity and that it should be excluded from the list of *alleged* crimes."[23]

A couple of pages later I scribbled wildly in the margins: "This is second-phase Zionism." "This is not ethnic cleansing." There is a "necessary, useful distinction between transfer and cleansing." "The commonplace of transfer in WWII and after ..." "If you see this through the imagery of war ..."

That is how I missed the cry of outrage and sorrow that had inspired the historian's words.

Now I am reading Nur Masalha's *Politics of Denial,* and I am listening; I am trying to hear, and I am hearing:

"The children were killed by breaking their head with sticks."[24]

Here was the type of image I had lost in my journey through abstractions. The children were killed by breaking their heads with sticks? Did I just read that? It is the testimony by Israeli soldiers present in 1948. And now what am I going to do with it? Children killed with sticks? That cannot be in the name of security, that cannot be justified by acts occurring in war time, can it?

> One commander ordered a sapper to shut two old women in a certain house ... and blow up the house ... One soldier boasted that he had raped a woman and then shot her. One woman, with a newborn baby in her arms, was employed to clear the courtyard where the soldiers ate. She worked a day or two. In the end they shot her and her baby.[25]

These testaments are not made by enemies of Israel; they are made by her soldiers, men who witnessed these events, in 1948. They can be found in the Israeli archives; anyone who is interested can have a look and doubt or verify for herself the authenticity of the reports. More accessible still, the books I have piled up around me on the floor (see For Further Reading). If I am an example of a certain kind of Jewish reader, the study of the archives will not do us much good when we are determined not to know what the archives are telling.

Yosef Nahmani, director of the Jewish National Fund office in eastern Galilee between 1935 and 1965, recorded in his diary (November 6, 1948) this briefing from Israel's Minority Affairs Ministry. Members of the ministry were discussing "the cruel acts of our soldiers" in 1948:

> In Safat, after ... the inhabitants had raised a white flag, the [soldiers] collected and separated the men and women, tied the hands of fifty-six *fellahin* [peasants] and shot and killed them and buried them in a pit. Also, they raped several women ... in Saliha ... they had killed about sixty-seven men and women. At Eilabun and Farradiya the soldiers had been greeted with white flags and rich food, and afterwards had ordered the villagers to leave, with their women and children. When the [villagers] had begun to argue ... [the soldiers] had opened fire and after some thirty people were killed, had begun to lead the rest [toward Lebanon] ... Where did they come by such a measure of cruelty, like Nazis? ... Is there no more humane way of expelling the inhabitants than such methods?[26]

An Israeli minority affairs minister has compared the soldiers of the IDF to Nazis. Can I answer him by talking about identification with the aggressor? The concept has always troubled me for the way it contains a measure of justification. Its explanation rests on the knowledge of prior victimization undergone by the current perpetrator. Behind his violence we are invited to remember the atrocities he has undergone. Surely the minister is not saying that the soldiers of the IDF were Nazis. No identity has been established; it is the cruelty of both groups that is being compared. Bad enough. The whole thing sets my teeth on edge. I am writing my thoughts as fast as I think them and they keep trying to get away. I'm not sure why the government official is called a minister of minority affairs; during the time he occupied his office it was the Jews, not the Arabs, who were in the minority. This is of course one of the number disputes that erupt throughout the discussion. (How many villages, how many refugees, how many soldiers killed in the first months of the war, how many children beaten with sticks, how many Jews slain during the Arab Revolt?) Alan Dershowitz speaks of the number of Jews and Arabs within the area the UN had assigned to Palestine. He eliminates from the population tally of Palestine the Arabs of the West Bank and Gaza and "what is now Jordan." Were there really more of them than there were of us? Not according to this way of doing the numbers.[27]

Here we can see at work the way I use numbers to distract myself from what is really at stake. I am trying to entertain the idea of a comparison to the cruelty of Nazis. It is an effort of will to bring my mind back, to make myself ask the relevant questions. What accounts for this cruelty in a Jewish soldier? The government official who asks might have answered his own question.

Men come to acts of cruelty and brutality of this kind because they have learned to see their neighbors with contempt. It begins with a sense of superiority derived from birth and origins. The other is lesser, insignificant, uncivilized, not entitled to the rights we claim for ourselves. We despise these dark(er)-skinned neighbors not just in warfare, but daily, as we go about our lives. "It would have been better, perhaps, if there were no Arab students. If they remained hewers of wood it would perhaps be easier to rule over them."[28] This, from a Jewish man.

A camp commander is speaking through a loudspeaker to his Palestinian captives: "You are a people of monkeys. You are terrorists and we will break you. You want a state? Build it on the moon. Whoever causes trouble here, will be shot."[29] These men have not been tried or condemned. It's impossible to know if they are terrorists, but we know that they are not monkeys.

An Israeli officer of the military government in the West Bank drives up to a government building, blowing his horn and shouting at a guard. Raja Shehadeh, a Palestinian lawyer, writer, and human rights activist, describes the following scene.

> "How often must I tell you that I don't want anyone in the driveway? Let them stand on the side. It is not a parade here."
>
> The officer's eye fell on a young well-built man leaning on a tree, smoking a cigarette. He didn't like his open and bold expression. "What are you standing there for?" he asked.
>
> "I'm waiting to collect my ID," the man said without removing his cigarette.
>
> "Take away your cigarette when you speak to me. What's your name?"
>
> "Mahdi Hammad."
>
> "I will remember your name and we'll see if you get your card today. You must learn manners first."[30]

You must learn manners first? To whom does he think he's speaking? An insubordinate, a prisoner, a child, an animal in training? Mahdi Hammad is standing in line to comply with Israeli military orders. Because he is smoking a cigarette he won't be able to get his ID. Not today, perhaps not tomorrow? Without his ID he can't get work; he can't pass through the Israeli check-points. Is this roughness and brutality the inevitable fate of an occupying army? I wish I could say yes and leave it at that. But the problem goes further back.

Shortly after the founding of Israel, at a state meeting, an Israeli minister speaks about Arabs. The minister's treatment of the Arab refugees is so shocking to a visiting British member of parliament that the discussion has been set down and can be found in the parliamentary record. "'Doctor Hacohen, I am pro-foundly shocked that you should speak of other human beings in terms similar to those in which Julius Streicher spoke of the Jews. Have you learned nothing?' I shall remember his reply to my dying day. He smote the table with both hands and said, 'But they are not human beings, they are not people, they are Arabs.' He was speaking of the Arab refugees."[31]

It must weigh heavily on a Jewish reader to discover that this is not an isolated incident. "According to one of his biographers, David Ben-Gurion refused to accept his new Israeli ID card because it was printed also in Arabic—one of Israel's two official languages ... Golda Meir said ... whenever she heard an Arab mem-ber of the Knesset swear allegiance to the state she felt 'sick.'"[32]

What is the unthinkable thought trying to make its way through? It slips and twists, it tries to get away, the usual tactics. This passage snags and holds on tight: "The tragic irony is deep-ened by a fatal parallel. There is a symmetry between the Israe-lis' traumatic memory of holocaust and the neurosis of shame and anger, humiliation and white rage, that has been generated among Arabs by Israel's recurrent successes."[33]

I found this brave and daring when I came across it many years ago. Today, in pursuit of what I dare not think, I am invited (as Amos Elon has been in later writing) to take it further. The "fatal parallel" that makes of the Palestinians what we once were has not arisen from Israel's successes. It is our brutality that has brought it about. Catch this thought: *If we become like them, the people who wanted to exterminate us, to the degree that we become like them they have succeeded in destroying us.*

Why is the Israeli soldier kicking his Arab prisoner in the face? His prisoner is sitting on the ground, his hands tied behind him. Over and over again in the face. "His nose and face are covered in blood while the soldier continues to strike him."[34] Okay, yes: perhaps the thousands of years during which our people has endured persecution can help account for the way we have become brutal toward another people. Or perhaps the soldier cannot manage to see his prisoner as a suffering human being because he has been taught since childhood to see him as an animal. Daily, since childhood, he has been encouraged to see the Palestinians as "thieves, snakes, cockroaches and grasshoppers."[35] Colloquial Hebrew, filled "with expressions reflecting the prevailing prejudice" reflects this alienation. "'Arab' is synonymous with meanness, bad workmanship, and bad taste, as in 'Don't be an Arab,' 'Arab work,' and 'Arab taste.'"[36]

I don't want to believe that Jewish people think or talk like this, but the evidence is right here. And here too are my notes, written by me but almost illegible. I seem determined to hide from anyone else, and perhaps also from myself, what I have learned. My books have been stacked up, taken down, reassembled—as if the right arrangement could segregate the worst of what I am forced to know. And now, grabbing a book at random, opening it to a marked page, I find this: the messages sent to IDF soldiers by children born and raised in the settlements. One child asks the soldiers "to kill as many Arabs as possible." Another asks: " ... for me, kill at least ten." One child goes further: "Ignore the laws and spray them." Their teacher thinks these are examples of "healthy hatred."[37]

Can I imagine, under any circumstances, wanting my Jewish daughter to have written a letter like this?

What Did Ben-Gurion
Not Want to See?

Woe to them that are at ease in Zion
And trust in the mountain of Samaria.

Amos 6:1

I have worn a Star of David since I lived in Israel in 1971 at a time when I hoped to spend the rest of my life there. One day, in exasperation, I tugged at it, the chain broke, and the star landed on the floor at my feet. When I picked it up I realized that the points of the star were sharp, very sharp; I pressed them into my palm. My Jewish identity, my most profound sense of identity, was breaking up. It was heartbroken. What had it meant to be a Jew? What had it meant to me, personally?

It began with the Pale and the pogroms, family stories; it included the near extermination of my people in the century in which I was born. It meant Ahad Ha'am, the cultural Zionist who believed in a binational Palestinian/Jewish state. It meant Freud and Einstein and Emma Goldman, who reminded me of my mother; the German-Jewish poets Else Lasker-Schüler and Gertrud Kolmar. Kolmar was transported to Auschwitz in 1943; she had refused to leave behind her ailing father who did not want to leave Germany. Conscripted for forced labor in an arms factory, silent for hours in an impenetrable isolation among the other workers, she composed poetry. The mystical poet Else Lasker-Schüler was driven out of Germany, driven out of Switzerland; she wandered about in Jerusalem, her previous fame forgotten, reading her poetry to any gathering willing to pay her a small fee, writing her last play (*Ich und Ich*) on a crowded table in a room scarcely large enough to hold her bed.

Being Jewish included Kafka studying Hebrew, planning to settle in Palestine. (Kafka on a kibbutz?) And the conversions of Heine and Mahler, who nevertheless could not stop being Jews. Wrapped up in there was my admiration for Rosa Luxemburg who saw so early the dangers of the Bolshevik Revolution. Isaac Babel, riding as a conscript with the Cossacks but carrying an unloaded gun. All the left-wing, radical, socialist Jews I had known while growing up. My mother and her lifelong struggle on behalf of "the people." My gentle, tenderhearted father who imagined he would be a revolutionary when the time came. Studying Yiddish as a child, knowing what people were saying in Yiddish even before I began to study it. Carp in the bathtub at Passover. Eight candles. No Christmas tree. Compassion for the underdog. A people who for two thousand years had not gone to war, an ethical people allowed to quarrel with their God, a people whose own prophets could rebuke them, chastise them, call them to task when they strayed from righteousness. A people who, because of their suffering and persecution, had evolved a generous capacity for empathy.

For me, being Jewish had meant wearing a Star of David so that people would know I wanted them to know that I was Jewish in case they hadn't recognized me, even when I wasn't sure what being Jewish meant.

And then, one day, in the midst of my study and research, I no longer wanted to be Jewish. A woman with two Jewish parents, four Jewish grandparents, eight Jewish great-grandparents, all of them from Eastern Europe, from the Pale. Was there a choice? I got a new chain for my star. Now, when I wore it, it would be a promise to myself that I had taken in the wider meaning of being Jewish. If I was to remain Jewish, all that I didn't want to know I had to find out. The capacity for intimidation and violence, Ariel Sharon at the Temple Mount, Dr. Baruch Goldstein at the Tomb of the Patriarchs, Yigal Amir, who'd already had a career as a brutal soldier before he assassinated Yitzhak Rabin, his prime minister. My Jewish identity now had to include the concept of transfer, the Palestinian camps, the torture of prisoners detained without trial. These things of darkness. Not only because they were done in my name but because, in my ignorance and refusal to know, I had participated in their cruelty.

What is life like for the Palestinians in Judea and Samaria? A web of military orders governs their lives. "Military Order 1015, for example, prohibited the planting of any fruit tree or more than twenty tomato seedlings without the agreement and adherence to the conditions of the military government."[38]

Since I read this I have been trying to figure out what danger twenty-one tomato seedlings might have posed. Or what the punishment might be for planting one more seedling than permitted. Palestinians live with enforced closures of cities and towns, curfews, checkpoints, constant searches, house demolitions, the ever-present danger of being shot if they venture out of their homes during the hours of curfew.

"They have said anyone seen outside will be shot. One woman was hanging her washing when they shot her."[39]

I can see why I have not bothered to know these things. And now that I know, what now? The random arrests, the relentless confiscation of Palestinian lands. When villagers set out to pick olives in their orchards they are shot at by settlers armed with Uzis.

A woman named Rita, head of the Institute of Community and Public Health at Birzeit University, reports to a colleague about the behavior of the Israeli army: "They went into the ophthalmologic clinic of Medical Relief and destroyed all the big expensive machines and took away the patients' records. Now they even have our eye records." She wonders if anything can be done. Her colleague, a lawyer, thinks for a moment, then answers: "Nothing can be done ... Nothing at all."[40] I try hard but I cannot imagine how the destruction of eye machines will provide security to the Jewish people.

Wearing the Star of David must now mean: NO: this is not what it takes to found a state. NO: these are not things that can be justified because they happened in war. NO: security does not come before everything else. NO: our violence was not and is not only in our defense. This awareness: there is no perfect security; the effort to attain a security beyond breach will involve the sacrifice of tens of thousands of people who will be blamed for the insecurity. Surely, it must be their fault when the imagined security can never be attained. And this: the Palestinian people are not their leaders; their leaders are not the Palestinian people; nor are the suicide bombers or the armed terrorists who risk the civilian lives of their own people; the PLO is not the Palestinian people, nor is Hamas or Islamic Jihad. The Palestinian people are a people like us, peacemakers and killers, innocents and those whose hands have been bloodied, as have ours.

As an Orthodox Jew I would believe that we were driven from this land because of our sins. Therefore, a terrible question would confront me: is the Holy Land still promised to us if what we do on the land is not holy? "Woe to him that increaseth that which is not his! How long? ... Shall they not rise up suddenly that shall bite thee, and awake that shall vex thee ... Because thou hast spoiled many nations, all the remnant of the people shall spoil thee; because of men's blood, and for the violence of the land, of the city, and of all that dwell therein." These are the words of Habakkuk, and they have not lost their prophetic vigilance.

As a woman of the twentieth century I have learned that the end cannot liberate itself from the means. What we have done to realize the dream is what we have, is all we have, when we arrive at the goal. There is no magical moment when the warrior god lays down his arms to lie down with the lamb. What is a Palestinian refugee camp like? It's stunning to realize I never bothered to wonder before. Nor have I understood the refugees' stubborn (as I saw it) refusal to be resettled somewhere else. The Palestinians practice *somoud* (perseverance), the outstanding virtue of the exile who cannot renounce his homeland. Cannot? Will not? Must not? In spite of conditions like these:

> Thousands of families were still living in whatever makeshift shelters they had been able to find in the midst of the war—unfinished buildings, stores and warehouses, huts, plastic tents, and improvised shelters made of whatever materials were available. A few sporadic faucets in the streets provided water to long lines of women and children. A sickening stench rose from the orange groves and empty lots that had been functioning as outhouses for the past five months. The gloomy November air was filled with suffocation, dirt, and despair, and the first rains that had fallen had already hinted to the poor refugees what was awaiting them when winter would come.[41]

These people are waiting to go home, longing for Palestine the way we have longed for our land for thousands of years, with a memory even more bitterly acute because more recent.

> I was raised under an olive tree,
> I ate the figs of my orchard
> Drank wine from the sloping vineyards
> Tasted cactus fruit in the valleys—more, more.
> The nightingale has sung in my ears
> The free winds of fields and cities have always
> touched me
> My friend
> You cannot ask me to leave my own country.
>
> —Fouzi al-Asmar[42]

What if, over the years, instead of reading books of facts, struggling with numbers and heated debates, I'd been listening for Palestinian voices?

> You cannot imagine the pain of going back to your childhood home, of seeing your orange groves as you remembered them, heavy with ripe fruit. You cannot know the agony of seeing other people manhandling your trees and of knowing that you are a stranger there, forbidden to touch even one orange.[43]

A people has emerged where before there were only the ghostly dwellers of an empty land. Why would I have cared to know how these people who were never there were now living?

> Nobody who has ever visited a Palestinian camp can forget the things he has seen or the desperation he has sensed: the squalid sheds, their roofs of tin or corrugated iron,

weighted down with stones to stop them blowing away; the walls of squashed petrol cans, a few plants growing in rusty tins, the clouds of flies, the stink of animals and excrement; the long lines of women, queuing up for rice, or kerosene or a few kilos of flour; above all the faces, of women, worn and vacant, exhausted by years of carrying water and heavy loads, of children, wide-eyed and dirty.[44]

Ben-Gurion never wanted to know how the Palestinians lived. He never visited an Arab town or village from the time the State of Israel was proclaimed. He refused, on a visit to the Jewish town of Upper Nazareth, to visit Arab Nazareth, a few hundred meters away.[45] What was it he didn't want to see or know? Is this act of refusal akin to the avoiding that has driven my ignorance all these years?

This question perplexes me; I turn it over and over. It makes me think of the two-thousand-year-old Jewish identity crowding Ben-Gurion when he was unable to visit Arab Nazareth, the identity of a people who do not engage in combat, who see themselves with pride as a people who abhor any form of violence. Perhaps he feared that what he saw would eat its way into that old-world Jewish heart he was trying to disown. This man, building a state, creating a nation for his people, could not eliminate the values he had inherited with his history. Was Ben-Gurion afraid to take in what the founding of our homeland had meant to the people we displaced? Was he fighting off the presence, still perhaps alive and active within him, of those Jews who would have seen in this exiled and dislocated people an image of themselves?

In my childhood I have suffered fear, hunger, and humiliation when I passed from the Warsaw Ghetto, through labor camps to Buchenwald. Today, as a citizen of Israel, I cannot accept the systematic destruction of cities, towns, and refugee camps. I cannot accept the technocratic cruelty of the bombing, destroying and killing of human beings … I hear "dirty Arabs" and I remember "dirty Jews." I hear about "closed areas" and I remember ghettos and camps. I hear "two-legged beasts" and I remember "*Untermenschen* [subhumans]." I hear about tightening the siege, clearing the area, pounding the city into submission and I remember suffering, destruction, death, blood and murder … Too many things in Israel remind me of too many other things from my childhood.[46]

There are so many things I have not known about Palestinian lives. A people who, in their poverty and unemployment, are more heavily taxed in Gaza than our people in Israel. And yet, they are a people who value education the way we Jews value it. In the poorest families "there is always one brother working hard to educate his siblings and give them the chance of a good profession and a better life."[47] A people who, in exile, continue to think of themselves as coming from the villages where their parents and grandparents were born. In the Gaza Strip "villagers sought one another out in the tent camps, until the old neighborhood took shape in their new location, reproducing the same divisions and loyalties as before."[48] There are still distinctive village traits, a tendency to be a fast-talker never at a loss for words if your parents or grandparents came from the village of Majdal; an inclination to take pride in the prized grapes of a village never seen; memories passed from parents to the next generations, "down to the colors of the wheat and corn, the sight of the plums and oranges … the smell of the fertile earth."[49] In the village of Hamama lovers would meet under the apricot trees, a father tells his daughter, who has been born in the camps, "in a concrete forest with improvised tin fences and alleyways riven by ditches running with sewage." There is no fruit in the camp, but when the daughter remembers her parents she can picture the figs and the golden apricots. The people from Majdal, whom we imagine as our enemies, with daily lives intent on our destruction, were once regarded by other Arabs as the "Jews of Palestine" because of their learning.[50]

For a long time I didn't realize that Palestinian terrorists occupy Palestinian civilian camps, looking for a safe place from which to attack the IDF, with no regard for the lives of the people they claim to represent. A child goes out for ice cream into a quiet street in Gaza. Some soldiers emerge from a side street. She runs and is shot in the head with a rubber bullet. She never recovers the control of her muscles. Her name is Lulu, a nickname we too had for our daughter when she was a little girl.[51] How easily I can remember her, my own child, running out for ice cream and coming back home safely. That is the way I must begin to think: comparatively, humanely, sympathetically. I must imagine myself as a Palestinian mother. No one is providing for the development of my neighborhood; the available education lags behind the number of children who need to be educated. The streets are pitted, the water is scarce and tastes foul, the electricity is turned on and off by the whim of another people's army, sewage runs in the streets, the telephone frequently does not work. My children are in constant danger, stepping out for ice cream, going down the street for a bottle of milk, standing on a street corner watching the neighborhood boys throw stones at tanks. In some years, a child under the age of six is shot in the head once every two weeks. I cannot begin to imagine what it is like to be a Palestinian mother, but I am trying.

If I was once inclined to imagine her always at work plotting against our people, I am now willing to know how much she is occupied with her own life. Where would she find the time to attack us? Raising five children in a society where large families are desired no matter how great the family's poverty, taking in sewing to support a family with an absent father, cleaning other women's houses, being looked down on by the native Gazans, who have contempt for the refugees, getting food into the house, cleaning the house, cooking, shelling peas, making sure the children are doing their homework.

> *On windy days a woman drives to the shore early in the morning. The beach is empty. She finds a secluded spot, and far away from other people "she turns her face to the sea and screams into the wind."*[52]

Ben-Gurion once vigorously believed "in the possibility of reaching an accord with the Arabs." Differences between the two peoples, he argued, could be settled through heart-to-heart discussion between their leaders. We are told by his biographer that "[he] emerged from these conversations [with Arab leaders] disappointed and more soberly realistic than he had been before."[53] Disappointed, but still the man who had so recently believed in the heart?

Have we all become little Ben-Gurions, warding off an aching Jewish guilt toward the Palestinians, a people in many ways so much like ourselves before we gained a homeland? This is a people for whom we would imagine feeling the most intense kinship, whose plight we would be eager to relieve, whose suffering would remind us of our own. It doesn't make sense that we Jews can live so comfortably, in our expensive Israeli cities with their tattoo parlors and discos, sushi bars, upscale neighborhoods and art galleries, while only miles away there are the wretched conditions we help to perpetuate. It doesn't make sense unless we can persuade ourselves that every one of these people is an enemy, intent on killing us and destroying our state. Every last one of them? No innocents among them?

We say we are building a wall for our security. Perhaps we are building it to maintain our ignorance.

Maybe when we insist on the need for security, although we have the fourth-largest army in the world, and when we justify so stridently the violence of our behavior during war, or refuse to acknowledge the catastrophe that has befallen the Palestinians, or the role we have played in bringing it about, and when we refuse to consider any kind of reparations or apology, we are shouting down the old Jew, still alive in us, who is ashamed of us.

Amos Kenan, a journalist, has recorded an instance of this divided Jewish identity. As a soldier during the Six-Day War he observed the destruction of Palestinian houses and villages by the Israeli army. "We didn't let them return to the village to get their belongings, because the order was that they were not allowed to see their homes being destroyed."

There were soldiers present who had no objection to the demolitions, but some soldiers wept. They distributed water from a military vehicle, along with candy and cigarettes. Other soldiers began to cry. "None of us could understand how we Jews could do this." [54]

This question, that must never sleep, has kept me up on many nights. How can we understand that Jews could do this?

VII

The Gift of Not Looking Away

David Shulman, an Israeli professor at the Hebrew University of Jerusalem, is a member of the peace group Ta'ayush. Members of this group, both Palestinians and Israelis, cross through blockades and checkpoints to help rebuild houses on the West Bank. They carry blankets to displaced people who have lost their homes. They help villagers threatened by settlers gather olives from their groves. Ta'ayush means "living together."

I am reading Shulman's description of this peace movement because I want to know what it takes to be an activist of this kind, a member of the loyal opposition, dedicated to nonviolent action in the face of violence. Joining them through reading is an act of imagination, nothing more, but perhaps I will find out where I might follow and where I might lose heart.[55]

The group arrives, against the ever-present threat of arrest and violence, to clear a village aqueduct that has been blocked at one end by the Jerusalem municipality. The municipality has also put in a large cesspool at the other end, below the aqueduct. This aqueduct used to carry clean spring water. The villagers have wanted to unblock the channel and restore the fresh water, but they have been afraid. The members of Ta'ayush arrive to help them and to protect them from the police. They are also there to oppose the municipality's plans to demolish eighty-eight houses in al-Bustan. The municipality intends to eliminate the entire Arab neighborhood, some one thousand people rendered homeless. Teams of volunteers, Palestinian and Israeli, clear away the debris, the broken branches, the piles of moldy plastic. They break up the caked soil below the aqueduct, carry buckets with rocks and earth to build up a terrace.

This is peace work, visionary and compassionate; it makes a claim on a future that might possibly, just possibly, reflect its values. I would like to participate in making a future of this kind, but the work is dangerous. Here, in places like Chavat Maon, Itamar, Tapuach, and Hebron, the settlers have been given freedom to terrorize the local Palestinian population. They have been known to attack, beat, shoot, injure, and even kill in the name of a biblical teaching, two millennia old, that Jews have a right to this land, an exclusive right to it.

The members of Ta'ayush gather on a winter day to bring blankets to several thousand Palestinian herders and farmers, people who survive on a dry and stony soil by tending the few small patches of ground where cultivation is possible. They are cave dwellers who have been in the hills south of Hebron since the 1830s. Between July 3 and July 5, 2001, the caves were attacked and destroyed by a military operation; wells were blocked, flocks liquidated, hundreds of families expelled. The cave dwellers have never engaged in violent acts; they are a peaceful, civilian population with a way of life that evokes ancient, biblical virtues; it is as if they have been here all along, as if they belong to the place. Amos Elon writes that "many young newcomers at first tended to see the Arab felahin in the almost biblical simplicity of their lives, as direct descendants of the ancient Hebrews."[56] Shlomo Lavie, a member of the second wave of settlement, visited two Arab villages near Jerusalem in 1906, and wrote, "It is certain that their inhabitants are descendants of the ancient Jews."[57] Is envy of their long tenure a reason so much settler violence is directed against them?

Nevertheless, it is illegal to bring them blankets. The effort to help is an act of civil disobedience, and it has costs. Arrest is possible. Violent attacks are commonplace. An eighty-two-year-old Palestinian mother is out herding sheep on her family's land when a settler shows up and threatens her. Ta'ayush members who rush to help her are shot at by the settler, who beats the screaming woman on the head with a rock.

As I read, I ask myself, would I have come rushing to help her? And how would I fare at the end of this story when, as always, the settler goes free, neither chastised nor prosecuted? In situations like this, would I be able to remain nonviolent? I carry these stories with me when I leave the book, weighing my moral stamina, testing an imaginary courage. If I got angry enough I would be brave—that is how I have always overcome fear—so why would this be any different? But courage dredged up out of rage will easily turn violent. Is that what I would be as a member of this group, a woman who couldn't keep herself from picking up a stone and hurling it?

Shots ring out. The caravans of Chavat Maon, inhabited mainly by young men, are on the hill nearby; now down the hillside they come in skullcaps and tzitzit fringes, shooting. A member of the peace group hears a bullet pass over his head. One of the settlers has perfected a sling. He hurls rocks at the group; they whistle past like missiles, obviously lethal. "You should be ashamed," they scream. "What kind of Jews are you?" Shulman shouts back: "I am a Jew. That's why I am here."[58]

I can imagine the way I too would shout, accusing them of destroying Judaism, of forcing me to take them in, the worst imaginable shadow, as part of what it means to be a Jew. As I read, a hatred potent as the hatred I see in their faces enters my mouth:

You call yourself Jews? You are vicious, violent, righteous, out of control fanatics who have forgotten the most basic teachings of Judaism. I can imagine myself, down on the ground, brown soggy soil covering my fingers, reaching for the nearest stone. A member of the peace group is crying out to remind us not to respond to violence with violence. I would become a liability to our group, a woman unable to control the rage their settler-rage calls up in me. I see my hand on the stone; in the instant I fling my arm back to hurl it at them, the difference between them and me dissolves. I am face to face with my double, my twin. I, who do not believe in violence even against ants, even against flies. "Undoing evil, the evil that comes from within—from yourself and your own people—is not simple."[58]

Another outing. I am thinking that men who beat old women with rocks would not hesitate to attack a Jewish woman who has come to help Palestinian villagers plow their fields. But this time, in my reading, I am strangely removed from the threat of violence. All I can think of is how fine it is to be up high in the hills when the village elders are planting barley seeds. As a young woman I went to Israel to learn how to work the land; if I had stayed would I have been able to take this kibbutz idealism out into the killing fields in defense of my Palestinian neighbors? One deserves to be kept up nights with a question like this.

"To watch the destruction—self-destruction—of an entire world, you need only ordinary eyes and the gift of not looking away."[59] I have not been gifted with this ability, but I am determined to acquire it. I am trying to make "ordinary eyes" from eyes that have systematically looked away. Shulman remembers the lessons his mother taught him when he was a child: "because we were slaves in Egypt, we understand, we feel, we imagine, we will never hurt those who are oppressed."[60]

These teachings are another voice in the Jewish narrative.

Amira Hass heard them too: "My parents' memories, told to me since my childhood and absorbed by me until they became my own, are the other part of the story. Holocaust survivors, communists, southeastern European Jews living in Israel, my parents had raised me on the epics of resistance, on the struggles of a persecuted people."[61]

The same stories and teachings were imparted to me in childhood by my mother and father. And so I ask: Is it too late? Still possible? Do we even care to regain the Jewish voice that spoke these stories, taught them, and held them as self-evident?

There is no magic in learning to see. It takes a willingness to call up the still-remembering Jewish heart that could never hurt those who are oppressed. A determination to feel my way into the meaning of that oppression as it is now experienced by another people, the scope and size and scale of it. A willingness to right some false impressions.

Some very, very false impressions.

And so I find myself at the end of a warm day in late summer fastening a net around a tree from which raccoons have been tearing down the unripe apples. I am at home, in California. More than thirty years have passed since I left the kibbutz, but the questions in my mind today are driven by memory and anguish. I throw the net over the small tree, tie two edges together, and wonder why I have always believed that the violence of a suicide bomber is so much worse than the violence of uniformed soldiers attacking a civilian town to root out terrorists. I always thought it was a question of numbers, but it turns out this is not the case. Statistics have been available for a long time from B'Tselem, the Israeli Information Center for Human Rights in the Occupied Territories.[62] It is clear from the numbers reported on the B'Tselem Web site that between September 29, 2000 and February 23, 2009, the deaths of Palestinian children far outnumbered the deaths of Israeli children. During that period, 123 Israeli children were killed by Palestinians and 1,487 Palestinian children were killed by Israelis. Nevertheless, I can't get the image of the suicide bombers out of my mind. The hot, windless Mediterranean day, a mother and her fifteen-year-old daughter out shopping after school. A bomb goes off next to their car.

A girl cries out. (This is a direct quote. I copied it from a newspaper, but didn't note the source.)

> People coming apart o my god right in front of us all over the place. O my god, o my god, Mama gets out of our car. Mama steps on a finger. Let us get out of here Mama, let's go, let's run, let's get away. If you walk in the street you will fall, you will slip in the blood.
>
> Mama says we have to help them, Mama says never take the bus, walk everywhere we have to go. Could happen, any day, any minute, look around, look over your shoulder, keep an eye out. That is me, screaming no no no no no no no. That is me shouting get them, get them, make them stop, do something, kill all of them. (June 19, 2002)

We venture out into the world as an act of faith, because we love life and want to participate in it and because we have come to trust in the ordinary. I used to think it was the terrorists who were responsible for the annihilation of everyday life. Now that I am trying to see with "ordinary eyes," I see this differently. B'Tselem reports that in this same period 1,072 Israelis and at least 6,348 Palestinians were killed and 8,864 Israelis and 39,019 Palestinians were injured. The suicide bombers and the terrorists are killing and maiming fewer people than are maimed and killed by our army? If you drop a bomb on a building, even a hospital or kindergarten, most of the people inside will be blown away without a trace. Is that what it comes to? If I am not told of the blood in the street, the bodies flying apart, if I don't imagine the physical horror, I don't have to believe in it and I don't feel it?

My eyes had been fixed exclusively on the Israeli casualties. These numbers turn everything inside out. The vertigo of a worldview suddenly toppled. Who is the aggressor? Who is the victim? Sometimes I feel as if I am rewriting myself.

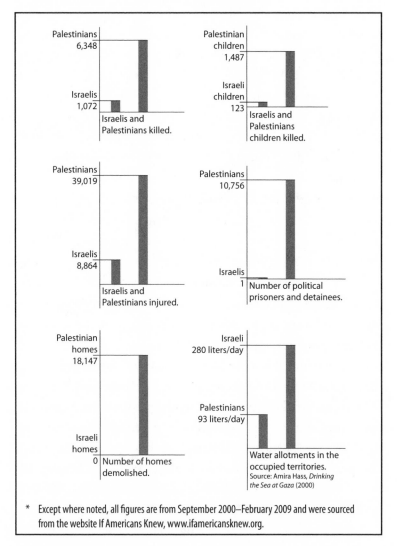

* Except where noted, all figures are from September 2000–February 2009 and were sourced from the website If Americans Knew, www.ifamericansknew.org.

We imagine the first three months of the First Intifada as a time when rocks were thrown at Israeli soldiers, settlements were shot at, and military installations and settler roads in the occupied territories were attacked.

As it turns out, during those first three months, 279 Palestinians were killed, 82 of them children. I imagined a lot more casualties on our side, but in the same period of time, 41 Israelis were killed, and none of them were children. All but four were killed inside the West Bank and Gaza. Before the intifada's first suicide bombing took place inside Israel, 149 Palestinians had been killed in the occupied territories.[63]

I am reminded of those cunning double drawings. You start with an hourglass. You keep staring; an hourglass is all you see. Then suddenly, because you are concentrating, another picture emerges: the profiles of two women. What you see and what you could not see have always been there. Amos Elon has written that in the West Bank and in Gaza, the First Intifada was led by a few thousand teenagers and even younger boys and girls. They were armed with stones and slingshots, an occasional Molotov cocktail. Where we Jews have seen a ferocious enemy threatening our security, Elon sees a children's crusade. The occupied territories are filled with firearms, they are all over the place, it would have been easy to get hold of them. Yet, in three months of uprising the rioters did not fire a single shot.[64]

It's hard to believe that one can be so wrong about the world. Rock-throwing children where I'd imagined terrorists. Palestinians killed: 279. Israelis: 41. Palestinian children killed: 82. Israeli children: 0. The numbers are shouting: Wake up! Be curious! See!

The voice of David Shulman, a Jewish man who is capable of seeing: "I know, too, that I am seeing what can only be deadly real, the ground-level, human reality of attack, depredation, expulsion, the prelude to the vast expulsion that these Jews are planning for these people, all three million of them. Let no one say he did not know."[65]

Is that what we have in mind? Their expulsion? Are we making things so bad for them that they will want to leave? Gaza is very crowded. Amira Hass writes that 1,022,207 people live in the Gaza Strip, crammed together in its 147 square miles. It is the most densely populated area in the world. When the settlers were there, 20 percent of that territory was off-limits to Palestinians.[66]

These numbers need no embellishment. They can be twisted and turned but they cannot be denied. They are as close to facts as we can ever come. We dare not look away from them. Samir Abdallah, who lived in the West Bank, took part in the Oslo negotiations. He went on to head PECDAR (the Palestinian Economic Council for Development and Reconstruction). Studying the figures, he found that between 1967 and 1994 Israel had annually invested an average of $15 per capita in the Strip's infrastructure. In Israel, during this same period of time, $1,000 per capita had been spent.[67]

How should I imagine the daily lives of people living in this crowded space? These numbers have become another pair of eyes. In 1991, there was one telephone for every two people in Israel. In Gaza, one for every fifty. By 1995, there were 22,000 telephone lines in Gaza for a population of a million people. It can't have been easy to do business in a situation like this, where 1,040 out of the 1,909 commercial firms in the Strip (54 percent) were without telephone service at the end of 1992.[68]

Israel is in control of the water supply in the occupied territories. Water is scarce; it is rationed, and most of it goes to the settlements. In the occupied territories Palestinians receive an average of 93 liters per day per capita; Israelis living there receive 280 liters. Only 15 to 20 percent of the water supply that originates in the territories is consumed by West Bank Palestinians. The rest is transferred to Jewish settlers and to residents in Israel.[69]

A portrait is emerging through these numbers. A person suffering from an ethical blindness is being forced to see. I need all the help I can get. The absent people who were never there have acquired bodies and bodily needs. I begin to ask urgent questions. With so little water, how do they bathe? How do they wash clothes? What happens when they have no water to drink? Ibtisam Barakat, in a beautifully told memoir of her childhood in the West Bank, helps me develop the gift of not being able to look away.

Water: "Our drinking water came from a rain well in the backyard and was stored in a clay urn ... They watched over it carefully, snatching babies who crawled by it or shouting to warn children not to race near it."

Bathing: "The night before September 1, when my brothers began school, Mother bathed us all in a wide tin tub the way she did once every week."

Washing clothes: "Mother washed our clothes mainly on Fridays, when Father had no work and could drive us to a stream where many people gathered ... There, Mother met other women. Squatting or kneeling beside large piles of laundry, they used stones to rub the clothes clean. Then they built fires. In large tin cans they boiled the white pieces with a powder called Neeleh because it turned water blue like Al-Neel, the Nile River."[70]

Does this sound romantic, even nostalgic, a cliché of the happy country life? Mother and the women at the stream, the children bathing together in the tin tub, the precious clay urn that must not at all costs be broken. Looked at more closely it describes a life few Israeli Jews would be willing to live, in an impoverished country next to a prospering neighbor who has taken so much of the available water.

I don't have accurate numbers for how many Jews and how many Palestinians are in mourning, but I would imagine there is mourning over all the land, a mourning without borders, a lamentation slipping past the security blockades. A very old lamentation for this very old land. "Wailing shall be in all the streets; and they shall say in all the highways, Alas! alas! and they shall call the husbandman to mourning, and such as are skilful of lamentation to wailing. And in all vineyards shall be wailing" (Amos 5:16–17).

We are the daughters and sons of a prophetic tradition. A language has come down to us in which we can be troubled about Israel and darkly concerned about the behavior of our people. If only we are willing to see. Amos and Jeremiah and Haggai and Hosea were not self-hating Jews. We may have forgotten, but they understood that love for one's people can mean a refusal to turn away from difficult truth. It can mean chastisement: "O Israel, return unto the Lord thy God; for thou hast fallen by thine iniquity" (Hosea 14:1).

And rebuke: "Now therefore thus saith the Lord of hosts; Consider your ways. Ye have sown much, and bring in little; ye eat, but ye have not enough ... Consider your ways" (Haggai 1:5–7).

It can mean taking stock: "For the ways of the Lord are right, and the just shall walk in them: but the transgressors shall fall therein" (Hosea 14:9).

It can speak with outrage: "I will utterly consume all things from off the land, saith the Lord. I will consume man and beast ... I will also stretch out mine hand upon Judah, and upon all the inhabitants of Jerusalem" (Zephaniah 1:2–4).

It can threaten: "The great day of the Lord is near, it is near, and hasteth greatly, even the voice of the day of the Lord: the mighty man shall cry there bitterly" (Zephaniah 1:14).

And roar like thunder: "Woe to him that increaseth that which is not his! How long? ... Shall they not rise up suddenly that shall bite thee ... Because thou hast spoiled many nations, all the remnant of the people shall spoil thee" (Habakkuk 2:6–8).

It can admonish: "Woe to them that are at ease in Zion, and trust in the mountain of Samaria" (Amos 6:1).

It can lament: "For I have heard a voice as of a woman in travail, and the anguish as of her that bringeth forth her first child, the voice of the daughter of Zion, that bewaileth herself, that spreadeth her hands, saying, 'Woe is me now! For my soul is wearied because of murderers'" (Jeremiah 4:31).

This is a language of love, fire, and seeing. Traditional Jewish speech. We don't have to be prophets to see that our beloved homeland is in need of counsel. If not from us, the children of prophets, as only we can speak it, then from whom?

Prophecy is said to have ended when the Temple was destroyed. This cannot mean the First Temple, or Haggai, Ezekiel, Zechariah, and Malachi would not be called prophets. If prophecy ended after the Second Temple, when wisdom is said to have passed to the sages of the Talmud, we are following a descent from divinely inspired foreknowledge to the human capacity for wisdom and insight. To see, without turning away, to take in, without denying what one has taken in: this is a capacity any one of us might attain.

"Would that all the people of the Lord were prophets, and that the Lord would impart this spirit upon them." These are the words of Moses.

VIII

Lost in Translation

It's hard to think back to a time when I believed they were all terrorists. The number of terrorists among them is probably no greater than the number of those among us who want to see them transferred out of Israel/Palestine. Extremes of violence do not characterize either people. It is obvious by now that we too have our fanatics; no people has cornered the market on those. At one extreme, our settlers, the violence in our soldiers; at the other extreme, the members of Ta'ayush, Bat Shalom, the Israeli Committee Against House Demolitions. In between, the rest of us with our tragic capacity not to know what is happening to our neighbors. We have left the ranks of the persecuted and are now no different from other people who have the ability not to know, not to care, and not to feel.

Sixty years ago we conceived the warrior Jew: armed, muscular, formidably on guard to defend the homeland. But the Jewish "weakling" he was designed to replace can still be sensed in the extremism he is driven to embrace. "Death in combat is not the end of the fight but its peak; and since combat is a part, and at times the *sum total* of life, death, which is the peak of combat, is not the *destruction* of life, but its fullest, most powerful expression." This is Moshe Dayan, Israeli legend, military leader, and politician. He was the fourth chief of staff of the Israel Defense Forces, an epitome of the new Hebrew warrior. This is what he has written about his military experience: "Man goes to his death in battle not to bring salvation to others, not in order to sacrifice himself to the future; man goes to battle because he, personally, is unwilling to surrender, to be defeated: he does not wish to fight for his survival, but for him the content of his life and death is merely the supreme expression of the ferocity of his struggle."[71]

Deeply disturbing words, made even more so by their unwitting echo of Goebbels's diary entry for December 20, 1941, in which, similarly, war is characterized as the "highest expression of the life" of a people.[72] In Dayan, in all our celebrated warriors, as in Ben-Gurion, a Jewish identity that will not be erased continues to uphold traditional Jewish values. Two thousand years of exile and persecution are at work in this man who can only imagine destruction as life's fullest, most powerful expression. This is not strength; it is a terror of weakness, a tireless revolt against an exilic past he cannot escape. He imagines himself the new Jew, the warrior Jew, but is he? At the hidden core of himself we are likely to find the Jew he despises, his nemesis, the "weakling." Why else this bluster, this flight into violence, this elevation of warfare as the purpose and meaning of life? A warrior fights because he must, because he has a homeland and people to defend, not because violence best expresses his reason for existence. David, our warrior king, does not, even in the second psalm, his ferocious poem of revenge, praise violence for itself. The heathens will be scourged because they have set themselves against the Lord, and against his anointed. The Lord will laugh at them, their lands will be taken, they will be broken with a rod of iron, their bands will be broken asunder. They will be dashed in pieces like a potter's vessel. But when all this breaking and sundering is done, the Lord's king will return to his holy hill of Zion, to his wives and dancing girls, to his harp and his singing, as luxurious in peace as he has been mighty in warfare. David, the warrior, is a lover of peace; Dayan, our new warrior-Jew, considers death the fullest, most powerful expression of life.

As Jews, as a people, we are the inheritors of two histories, each with its own teaching: the often told story of our exile and persecution, and the older story of our conquest of Canaan. Would that the new Jew we were ambitious to create had absorbed the teachings of both. What a fine new human that would be, a bringer of peace from a position of power, its strength tempered by empathy, its force by compassion. Instead, as these possibilities are shaken up and sorted out, another people has been burdened with our recent history but not with the sacred duty imposed by the Talmud "to love and nurture and respect [humankind]."

Having undergone this bitter experience, the prolonged trauma of our being "strangers" in a strange land, shamefully exploited and persecuted, we were commanded in the Torah, not once but twenty-four times, to love the strangers among us, not to exploit them or put them to hard labor, to allow them to benefit from all our benefits: "And love the stranger because you were strangers in Egypt" (Leviticus 19:34).

"In the meantime," writes esteemed Israeli jurist Haim H. Cohn, "we were 'strangers' not only in Egypt, but in all countries of the Diaspora and of the exile. Not only were we strangers, there was no country in which we settled where we were not persecuted. ... It is this bitter experience that imposes on us the sacred duty not to do to others what others did to us, not to persecute any Gentile among us, any stranger who lives with us in our land, but to love and nurture and respect them."[73]

Look at our recent history. The parallels are staggering. Where once we were confined to ghettos, now we imprison others between walls. "We pass the chink in the wall that still allows people from Abu Dis to reach the hospital, Makassed, on the Mount of Olives. Old women, heavy in their thick black dresses, are painfully clambering across, over the rocks ... Soon this crack will be stopped up, and the only way to Makassed will be through Akr-Ram and the army checkpoints—a journey of several hours to reach a point less than a hundred meters away, but separated by the wall."[74]

Where once others obeyed orders to destroy us, now we obey orders to destroy them. "Then the critical sentence—almost unimaginable from Jewish lips—slips out: 'I [the commanding officer] am not meant to decide about the occupation, yes or no. I have my orders. I follow them as best I can.'"[75]

Where once we were vermin, they are now cockroaches. "When we have settled the land all the Arabs will be able to do about it will be to scurry around like drugged roaches in a bottle," says General Rafael Eitan.[76]

Where once we were exiled, we now compel others to live in conditions of exile. As we longed for this same land, our homeland, we have seen to it that they long for theirs: "Traditionally these were agricultural villages. Within a few decades the inhabitants have been intimidated, their life made unsafe and many of their fields expropriated, and they have been turned into construction workers building the settlements that stood on land that once had belonged to them."[77]

Murder without warrant, trial, or self-defense, as we too have known them. "Then she saw him: a blond man in his early twenties wearing a surgeon's mask. He looked like a young doctor prepping himself to take out someone's tonsils. [Her husband] tried to get off a shot but the young man coolly and without a word emptied the clip from his machine gun into [him]. Two more commandos emptied theirs before they all left. Not a word was said. A buxom female commando videotaped the execution."[78]

I omitted the name of the murdered man to leave open, if only for an eyeblink, the national identity of the blond man in a surgeon's mask. I found it hard to believe he was an Israeli.

We even have an ideology of national purity, in which the Palestinians have become the contaminant to our ideal of a pure Jewish state. Is there anything in our recent history we have not passed on to them? We, the chosen people, have we chosen them to live again through our history so that we can, at last, escape it?

When I lived in Israel I got something in my eye when I was working in the orchard. The eye swelled up and began to tear. I was driven down to the hospital, and after I was dropped off I made my way to the waiting area. I checked in at the desk and apologized in Hebrew for the need to speak English. I was told how and where to wait, also in English.

This is an old memory, and it may have done the sort of thing memory does in bringing together events that did not happen in the same time or place. I am certain that each happened in Israel, but when each happened I am not so sure. A bird came wildly into the waiting area, flew up to the ceiling, beat its wings against a wall, rushed toward the window, and crashed against the glass. We all looked as if we should have done something to help; there we sat, staring sheepishly at one another while the bird died and was swept away. The room filled up as we waited, each of us mildly interested as a new person came up to register at the desk. An old woman, her hands in agitation above her head, was trying to make herself understood. Everyone looked, a nearly perceptible shrug passed through the waiting room, of course no one could understand what she was saying. She was speaking Yiddish.

I looked around the room, expecting any number of people to come to her aid. No one stirred, everyone stared, the wild pantomime of hands and arms continued. Eventually, I found myself at the registration desk with my arm around her shoulders. She was no taller than my mother, who was, as an old woman, scarcely taller than a ten-year-old child. I didn't know what to say or what to do, so I told her, in Yiddish, that my name was Elke. There simply was not much more from my Yiddish-school days. Fortunately, communication does not depend on language; it passes easily through all sorts of barriers when one is desperate to understand. She was looking for her husband, who had been taken to the hospital in an ambulance. She hadn't been allowed to ride with him, and now she didn't know where he was. That, at least, is what I made out. I repeated this version in English to the young woman at the desk, who stared at the old woman and addressed her with painstaking annoyance in Hebrew. She was asking for the husband's name.

I vaguely remember a son or son-in-law arriving on the scene, but this is where the memory ends. It ends and comes back to me, comes frequently, over these many years. Recently, it has become persistent. What returns has something to say. What is it?

I have occasional dreams in which someone is speaking to me in Yiddish. I am struggling to understand, but my understanding begins to fray and I can only make out a few word-like sounds. It is like another recurrent dream in which I am trying to use a pay telephone but keep dropping and losing the coins. A desperate need to communicate, to understand, the means to do so falling away as I try.

The Jewish people used to have two languages.[79] For centuries we were a bilingual people, with a mother tongue (*mama loschen*) and a sacred tongue (Hebrew). Now our sacred language has become our everyday language, and we have lost our mother tongue. What have we lost along with it? I think about Yiddish and the sensibility of a Yiddish speaker. A gentleness, a stubborn sense of self-humor, a refusal to take oneself too seriously, a story-teller with the sort of playful kindness I saw in my father's family, his mother and father and eight brothers and sisters all native Yiddish speakers. What happens to a people when it loses its mother tongue? Does it lose along with it the mother qualities of compassion and empathy? Self-identification with strangers? A memory of Talmudic injunctions? A conviction that our suffering was to make us merciful? The Eastern Yiddish my family spoke was a "fusion language," built on a Germanic root but full of Russian and Hebrew words and words that sounded very much like German, which is probably the way I, an almost-fluent German speaker, was able to understand the old woman in the hospital. As a fusion language it guaranteed the speaker a certain kind of cosmopolitanism, if only to the degree that the Yiddish mouth was constantly involved with another people's words, mixing them in, sorting them out, rearranging and re-pronouncing them. Yiddish was an openhearted language, spoken by people who tended to be conversant with other languages. Over the centuries it had acquired the knack of absorbing untranslatable words, enriching itself with unexpected ways of saying things.

Yiddish carries the history of the Diaspora; it *is* the history of the Diaspora. As a language of exile it writes out on a speaker's sensibility an immediate knowledge of what it is like to be in yearning for a homeland. Yiddish is the language of being closed in, excluded, shut away, a ghetto language in which one knows what it is like to be despised and feared: a Yiddish speaker is one who is said to contaminate wells, to use the blood of Christian children to make the Passover matzoh. (This libel could still be dangerously brought, in 1928, against Jews living in America, in the small town of Massena in upstate New York.)[80]

Yiddish could have been the national language of Israel. It was widely spoken by the immigrants of the first and second Aliyah but was then discouraged when the state of Israel was declared in 1948. The government regarded Hebrew as Israel's official language and required all new immigrants to study and learn it. Or Yiddish might have been taught as a second language in the schools, as English is now. Why does this seem absurd? Is it because one simply cannot associate Israelis with the sensibility that produces a Yiddish speaker?

No wonder the memory of the old woman keeps returning. A bilingual people has lost one of its languages and with it perhaps the capacity to feel empathy for the Palestinians and for its own old people. Is a people without a mother tongue no longer capable of compassion?

> His attacker then rushed at him, threw him to the ground, and smashed at his skull with the barrel of his M16 rifle, opening a deep gash ... another batch of settlers, most of them in their white Shabbat clothes, has suddenly appeared and is closing in on the rest of us. Two of them are carrying long clubs; another starts hurling rocks at us [at members of the peace group Ta'ayush] ... Some of these [are] young settler women, who have joined their men on this pleasant Shabbat afternoon outing. These women seem to relish the sight of blood. As for the men, the faces of those closest to me—religious Jews with skullcaps, most with beards—are disfigured by the chilling presence of undiluted hate.[81]

I cannot imagine these people speaking Yiddish. I just cannot imagine it, even if they do.

Oasis of Peace

Is it really so hard to admit that "they" are more like us than we care to acknowledge, more like we were than we care to remember? How long, I wonder, will we be able to stifle our compassion for these people who live in unlivable conditions on the borders of our flourishing state? Perhaps, because we cannot image where this compassion would take us, we cannot allow ourselves to feel what we otherwise might naturally feel.

Many of us have heard by now about Neve Shalom/Wahat al-Salam and its radical experiment in communal living by people who might otherwise be considered enemies. Few of us will have studied carefully its recipe for resolving conflict. Bruno Hussar, who founded Neve Shalom/Wahat al-Salam, was born in Egypt in 1911 to nonobservant Jewish parents. By the time he came to Israel in 1953 he'd been around; he'd held first Hungarian, then Italian citizenship and lived for many years in France, where he had converted to Catholicism and joined the Dominican Order. His mentor, Father Avril, hoped to establish a center for Jewish studies in Jerusalem and thought that Bruno, a Jew by birth, would be the right man to undertake this mission.

Arrival in Israel brought with it the conviction that he was a son of the land, living among his own people, in his own country, although the civil authorities did not regard him as a Jew. From 1953 to 1959 he ministered in French, English, and Italian in Jaffa and became active in an organization to establish relations and reconciliation between Christians and Jews. From 1964 to 1970 he was active in numerous ecumenical associations, and in 1968 he was sent by the Israeli Ministry of Culture on missions around the world. Then, in 1970, he acted on an old dream. He wanted to participate meaningfully in bringing peace to Israel/Palestine. He would establish a community where Arabs and Jews could live together in peace and harmony. It would be called Neve Shalom/Wahat al-Salam—the Oasis of Peace.

It is not easy to place a dream of this kind in the scale of large and small. From one point of view, in terms of the difficulty realizing it, this is a big dream. And it is big also in its utopian vision of brotherhood between two embattled peoples. From another point of view, from that say of bringing peace to the Middle East, reassuring the Israeli people about their security, resolving the Palestinian refugee question, it isn't much at all. Even if fully realized, what would it be when measured on this larger scale? A single community, a little village somewhere, with a handful of people struggling to live in harmony together? Leaving aside the question of whether such a dream was attainable, would it matter if it were?

As a woman trying to learn, trying to listen, trying to see, I am interested in the village. I am also interested in the process of translating a dream into reality; I want to know more, as much as I can, about the state of mind that makes it possible. I am reading *Oasis of Dreams* by Grace Feuerverger—a rare and wonderful opportunity to enter this visionary world. Feuerverger presents the many voices of Neve Shalom/Wahat al-Salam, from interviews with the founders and administrators to conversations with participants in the School of Peace—all of them thoughtful people who are concerned about the world and aware of participating in an important experiment. (All of the quotations in this chapter are from her book.)[82]

The village's founder, Father Bruno, is an articulate and wise man with a gentle sense of humor and a deep faith and compassion. Where, for instance, do you get a piece of land when you don't have money and you don't have influence? And how do you keep going when your inquiries turn out to be fruitless, when promises are made and hopes are dashed? It helps, of course, to be a man of conviction, gripped by a powerful vision. It helps too that you can draw to your purpose warmhearted people of like mind. And it helps when one day, having heard of the enterprise, a Trappist monastery offers a hill to the little group with the dream. There is no reason to think of this gift as a miracle; it belongs to the energies set in motion by a strong visionary will.

But oh what an unpromising hill it is. Before the June war in 1967, it was a no-man's-land between Jordan and Israel, without water or a single tree, covered with brambles and stones, uncultivated since the Byzantine era. And of course no electricity. The hill has to be cleared, the roads made passable; there has to be water and a way for people to settle down and actually live their lives. This is the point where dreams collapse as the villagers run head-on into the prosaic. Here, the dreamers have to show themselves capable of hard work and tolerant of mundane tasks.

The first meetings to plan the village took place on this hilly land in its unredeemed state. The meetings were attended by Arabs and Jews from the neighboring villages and kibbutzim and by the Bedouin who were encamped in the area. They sang and danced and prayed and spoke in simple friendship, in the joyful spirit of beginnings that all such projects must have. Then, as they started to build the community, they encountered peculiar, unforeseen difficulties.

People arrived from all over the world to participate in the community—but they did not come from Israel. Not a single person, not a single family, neither Jewish nor Arab, came from Israel or from the occupied territories. Father Bruno had no wish to create a community for young people from all over the world who were looking for a better life. He wanted to create peace, he was dedicated to the land of Israel, he wanted specifically to bring its Arab and Jewish populations together in a way that preserved their individual cultural identities and helped them learn and understand their fellow-citizens. "Maybe in ten years there will still only be strangers on the hill, and then I shall probably have wasted my time," he reasoned. So he issued an ultimatum to God (and in so doing showed his decidedly Jewish origins? I think of Abraham when he took it upon himself to argue with God on the question of Sodom and Gomorrah). Father Bruno required two signs, or he would consider calling a halt to the experiment within a year. First: at least one family from Israel, whether Arab or Jewish, must come to build the community on the hill. Second: the community must get enough money to establish a "School for Peace."

This is another crucial moment. Father Bruno does not give up his original plan; instead, he holds fast to the specific nature of his dream and insists that God participate. He also understands that a great vision must be carried out in small steps. He does not ask for twenty or even ten families. He asks for one. God rises to the challenge, and why wouldn't he? What Creator could resist the muscular audacity of this dream? And so it comes to pass; a Jewish family from Beit Shemesh comes to live in the community. They stay for only a year, but others who knew them follow, a momentum starts, and the community begins to grow.

I am curious about this family. What if they had reasoned, as many of their friends must have, "Why should we tear up our lives for this little experiment that can never affect many people anyway? What can one family on a lonely, isolated hill possibly do to bring about peace?" Perhaps this family knew how to honor the first step, the small beginning. If despair keeps company with the impossibly large undertaking, faith, by contrast, lives companionably with small steps moving in the right direction.

The arrival of the family is, however, only the first answer to the challenge. What about the School for Peace? To solve this problem God must be prepared to step down into the world of the prosaic. Father Bruno's God is willing. He sends to the community a family from Switzerland. They have seen a television program about Neve Shalom/Wahat al-Salam, so they come for a visit. Immediately they understand, in their highly practical Swiss way, that the problem standing in the way of the dream is toilets. The community has been using a "bathroom of the saints"—a hole in the ground covered with a burlap sack. When the hole is full they dig another and move on. A hole in the ground may serve for saints and dreamers, but it can't be offered to their guests. Realizing this, the Swiss family endows the toilets, sends an architect to design them, and thus, in this highly concrete but divinely inspired form, makes a significant contribution to the goal of peace.

Of course, in an enterprise like this nothing is wasted; when gods get involved the most banal matter undergoes a significant transformation. The saintly holes become fertile earth where one day olive trees will be planted. The small, the prosaic, even the waste products are all essential in realizing a dream. It starts small, with a handful of people looking for a piece of land. It begins to grow, gathers people to it, exerts an influence. By 2000 there are forty families living in the village along with some single members. There are another three hundred families who wish to join. The school, which began with fourteen students, now teaches six hundred children, 80 percent of whom are drawn from surrounding villages. The school offers bilingual, bicultural, and binational education, taught by an equal number of Arab and Jewish teachers. More than twenty thousand adolescents from all over Israel and the West Bank have attended workshops at the School for Peace.

Let's listen to the kind of dialogue that takes place in the school.

An Arab participant: "You never legitimize what happens to the Palestinians. You always put us down. You see us as primitive, cruel, knife wielding. When will that stop?"

A Jewish participant: "Maybe we do put you down, but if we stop, you will do the same to us only more cruelly. If power will be in your hands, when they come to stab me—will you defend me?"

A Jewish student in a role-playing skit takes the part of a Palestinian mother who has just found out that Israeli soldiers have killed one of her children. "She began to cry and so did most of the participants. It was a pivotal moment. One Jewish boy blurted out in the silence of sorrow, 'Why choose that example? It's not very common.' Many Arab as well as Jewish peers retorted in disapproval. One Palestinian girl said, 'The fact that it happens is horrifying. Don't you understand that?'"

From a Palestinian participant climbing into the bus on the last day: "I saw what's behind the mask of my enemy. I think the process has to start from there."

A Jewish boy says about the workshop: "We saw that as Jews and Palestinians we shared a mutual need to have our pain recognized, or understood, by the other ... without feeling a need to compete over who suffers more."

Ahmed, the Palestinian facilitator: "The question of who is more of a victim, who is more guilty, who is more humane emerges and then unbearable feelings start to come out."

The workshops are designed to welcome, receive, and facilitate these feelings. Behind the mask of the enemy a suffering human being emerges, and listening becomes possible.

What's the recipe for this powerful undertaking?

You begin with a dream, add a handful of like-minded dreamers, fold in reverence for the prosaic with faith in the power of the small, and ask the divine to participate in stirring the mix until the great alchemical transformation can take place and the individual small steps and prosaic acts are transmuted into the dream's fruition. Dreaming big, starting small, respecting the steps, keeping on—which one of us, following this path, would not be able to achieve miracles?

But what about peace in the land of Israel?

The village, as a whole, practices and studies conflict resolution; it understands this in a radically simple way, for the village is "a place where people come from all over the country with a motivation of just learning to listen to one another." Just learning to listen. This seems deceptively easy and much too small to really count! Yet this listening to one another, as Father Bruno clearly sees, "is one of the most difficult things when you live in this kind of conflict." We can agree that it is difficult and acknowledge that it is worthwhile, but is this where our energy should go in our struggle for peace? Can it compare to the big steps being taken by the leaders of the United States, Palestine, and Israel?

Let's place these two visions side by side. The school in which listening is practiced; the world in which treaties are made. The school where hope becomes possible; the treaties that have consistently betrayed us into despair. A few years ago there was yet another troubled endeavor of the sort I've been watching since I was a child—a "road map," proposed by the United States, that hopes to bring resolution to the conflicts between the Palestinians and Israel. At first glance, it has all the earmarks of a carefully thought-out design, standing fully in the reality of the Middle East. Obstacles that might hinder the first steps are moved to later phases when they can be addressed more readily. In Phase I, all that the Palestinian leaders must do is control the violence of the intifada from their side. On the Israeli side, it requires only that Israel not continue with its settlement activity in the West Bank. This accomplished, Phase II will concern itself with establishing the Palestinian state, whose precise borders will still be open to discussion and negotiation. In the final phase, the questions of Jerusalem, the actual borders of the Palestinian state, and the Palestinian refugees will be discussed, negotiated, and resolved. Peace will reign.

All this sounds, indeed, a good deal more relevant and useful than people learning to listen to one another. After all, it concerns the great masses of people whose lives are affected by borders and the status of their cities, by the violence from which they suffer, and by the refugee camps in which they live. This road map was certainly seen by its proponents as an example of tough-mindedness leading to hard negotiations in the world of realpolitik. But how real could it possibly be? All the most difficult questions are postponed, the unanswered questions that drive the violence and make it impossible to contain. Israel has never agreed to return the territories occupied in 1967. The Palestinians have never agreed to renounce them. Israel has never been willing to discuss the return of the refugees to their homeland. The refugees dream of return. Israel has no officially declared borders; it is the only country in the world that has the theoretical ability to expand indefinitely. Meanwhile, the Palestinians are crowded into smaller and smaller spaces separated into cantons by "bypass" roads.

What's missing? Further negotiations, more phased approaches to a lasting solution? A different, even more punishing "fence"? Another promise from Hamas and Islamic Jihad? The trouble here is an inadequate sense of what makes things real. Raising the political issues and making plans for resolving them can only be as real as the ability on both sides to discuss the issues that are constantly being postponed. How many of us know that even under the Oslo process the Palestinians were granted autonomy and self-rule but not sovereignty? And when is the question of sovereignty to be raised, in the stage of final negotiations?

What might make the participants capable of this discussion now, when it might still have a chance to determine facts on the ground, is the very dialogue Father Bruno has in mind. And what would it take to make that dialogue successful? Perhaps, before all else, the ability to listen to your enemies and find out what their concerns are. This is the place where the small, the local, the concrete, the seemingly trivial (listening as compared to cease-fires?) shows its power as so much greater than the grandiose power of the large. Father Bruno had a brilliant insight that underlies the entire visionary undertaking of the village: Peace has to be taught and learned; the capacities for achieving and sustaining it have to be developed.

And so we return to the Oasis of Peace, this obscure little village thirty kilometers from Jerusalem, where forty families and some single people are working daily, every minute of their waking and dreaming lives, to understand one another, face their fears, express their bitterness, acknowledge their collective grief, face the sorrows of their collective past. This effort at conflict resolution takes place in the elementary school, where it is practiced by the children and their teachers; it occurs between the Palestinian and Jewish teenagers attending the School for Peace; it takes place in the governance of the village, between the equally balanced Palestinian and Jewish representatives; it is going on continually in the everyday lives of the families who inhabit the village and bring with them "the very human frailties and flaws" we would expect to find, even here.

It is the most realistic of attitudes—not merely the most profound, or visionary, or admirable, but simply the most realistic. What is being accomplished among the forty families of Neve Shalom/Wahat al-Salam is what is needed on a large scale, throughout the country and in all places of the world where conflict is destroying cultures and lives. The failed efforts of the Cairo Agreement, the Declaration of Principles and the Letters of Mutual Recognition, the Madrid Conference, the Oslo Accords and the permanent status negotiations, and the Washington Agreement have already written their own epitaph. What remains is reorientation and practice. We must start to practice what the villagers of Neve Shalom/Wahat al-Salam are practicing or face the fact (our one indisputable fact) that all our grand efforts are doomed to fail.

So let us take note: since 1991 the elementary school at Neve Shalom/Wahat al-Salam has been open to children outside the village. At present, there are more than six hundred children in the school. Moreover, tens of thousands of teenagers have gone through the School for Peace program. I have no trouble imagining that they have the potential to influence the future. I see them as thousands of individual glowing sparks seeded all over the land among their embattled peoples. Tens of thousands of glowing sparks that carry the lived experience of achieving harmony with people once imagined to be enemies. Very likely, one or ten or a hundred or even a thousand of them will become teachers and pass on to their students their recipe for resolving conflict. Another ten, perhaps, will refuse to serve in the occupied territories and will thus join and strengthen the refuseniks who are currently in prison for their acts of conscience. Others will tell their friends about the village and persuade them to attend the School for Peace and make the practice of listening part of their daily lives. The word will spread and the habit will grow, and who is to say that this grassroots effort will take longer to bring about peace than the ever-aborted agreements and treaties and cease-fires?

The solutions to problems between peoples are not going to come about through agreements and cease-fires and accords, all these steps that sound so plausible, seem so real, would appear to be so cogent politically, but which ignore the "small" and fundamental things required to bring about change.

Realpolitik has been steadily failing since the 1940s and will continue to fail precisely because it doesn't have a sufficiently complex view of reality—one that requires fundamental change on the part of the participants so they can hold to the agreements on which everything depends.

It is getting dark; I have taken refuge at the outskirts of the village, as I imagine it, to gather my thoughts at a time of long shadows and turning homeward. I remember the day in summer camp when I first heard about the new Jewish homeland; everyone jumped and clapped and shouted; a homeland just for us, for the Jews. Since then, I have come to believe that my people has done a great wrong to another people. This is not, it cannot be a fact; it is an expression of sorrow. If I were the voice of my people I would ask the Palestinians for forgiveness; I would look for a way to make reparations. Why should it be so difficult to speak these words—I see, I regret, I will repair—at the same time that we work ardently for the survival and well-being of Israel?

Small children, driving a pair of white goats with a stick, are running back into the village. I follow them. Their village collaborates with groups all over the world who are engaged in the work of resolving conflict by learning to listen to what people you might have regarded as your enemy have to say about the suffering and meaning in their lives. In 1997 Amin Khalaf and Lee Gordon, Israelis of Arab and Jewish origin, founded Hand in Hand. In 1998 the nonprofit organization opened an elementary school in Jerusalem and a second school in the Galilee; a third school was established in Wadi Ara in 2004. In 2007, the fourth Hand in Hand school opened in Beersheva. Over eight hundred students are now enrolled in the four schools; at least one new class is added every year. The schools are integrated, bilingual and bicultural, and fully egalitarian; each class is taught by one Arab and one Jewish teacher. The schools actively advocate social change and involve the parents as well as the children in a mission to create a countrywide network of such schools with a curriculum from kindergarten through twelfth grade.

Closer to home, there is *Tikkun* magazine and Rabbi Michael Lerner, from whom I had originally gathered the courage to think my way past the stories I'd been telling myself about Israel and Palestine. At the moments of my most extreme self-doubt, when I have asked myself if it is possible to passionately love Israel while still raising a voice of concern over the direction it has taken, *Tikkun* has been a crucial companion, reliably creating an atmosphere in which it is possible to think difficult thoughts. The journal, often a solitary voice within the American Jewish community, has withstood years of criticism and attack, transforming the way we allow ourselves to talk about Israel and heartening those who want to venture out beyond the established narrative.

It is easier for Israelis than for American Jews to combine love of country with an awareness of Palestinian suffering. The Jews of Israel have nothing to prove; they demonstrate their love by living there. I am thinking of the left-wing, religious organization Netivot Shalom. Its members demonstrate every Friday in front of the prime minister's residence; they carry signs that protest the occupation and the settlements. I admire this group for its dedication to the small; for the way, prior to Passover in 2002, they collected food and distributed it in Beit Omer, a Palestinian village near Hebron. They may, at present, be the only religious Zionist peace organization in the world.

On the Israeli side, the organizations working in the name of peace, listening, and nonviolent protest include Bat Shalom, Brit Shalom, the Israeli Committee Against House Demolitions, Machsom Watch, Peace Now, B'Tselem, Gush Shalom, HaKampus Lo Shotek, HaMoked, New Profile, Rabbis for Human Rights, and Yesh Gvul. On the Palestinian side, there are the Jerusalem Center for Women, the Palestinian Center for Rapprochement between People, the Palestinian Human Rights Monitoring Group, Miftah, the Sabeel Ecumenical Liberation Theology Center, the Hope Flowers School, and Alternative Palestinian Agenda.

There are also organizations in which Arabs and Jews are working together: Ta'ayush; the Alternative Information Center; Bil'in; Alliance for Middle East Peace; the Arab-Jewish Community Center; Arik Institute for Reconciliation, Tolerance, and Peace; Bustan; Hand in Hand; and Neve Shalom/Wahat al-Salam.

Smaller beginnings, smaller steps, a long path, a difficult journey. But this much we know: there are places in the world where, in the midst of violence and terror, people are living together in peace, even now.

So here I am, as the peace treaties come and go, lurching between hope and despair as I have for most of my life. Recently, I have made it a practice when the despair grows very big to remind myself of the saintly holes where olive trees are planted. I call to mind the two little girls in the Hand in Hand school who are inseparable. Areen, who is Arab, and Tahel, her best friend, who is Jewish. I think of Tahel's mother, who found it strange to visit an Arab home in Jerusalem's Beit Safafa neighborhood until her daughter started spending the night there. Now the mother too finds it perfectly natural. On the long, hard nights when I can't imagine any end to the violence in the Middle East, I imagine the two hundred Arab and Israeli schoolchildren who are sharing classrooms and learning one another's language. They, born to this violence, have every reason to despair, but they are not despairing; if they are not, I ask myself, what vision of the future do they have that they are not yet sharing with us?

X

Sinai-ism

What if all the Palestinians and all the Israelis who were tired of war decided to move together to some other place? What if, inspired by Neve Shalom/Wahat al-Salam, a call went out across the land to people who wanted to start over again? An enterprise of this kind is possible on a small scale, as we have seen. What if the small scale became a bit larger and moved across borders to a land that is truly without people? I am thinking of the desert—or rather, I am thinking of the desert as Palestinian and Israeli children might imagine it, a place waiting to be brought to life by a pioneering vision. It is a preposterous idea, of course, but is it any more preposterous than Zionism in the 1880s, when the idea of a Jewish state occurred to a handful of oppressed Jewish intellectuals living in the Russian Pale? It has all the advantages of a visionary enterprise; it sends out a call to the dreamers and those who cannot bear the conditions of their life. This time it will not be a state for a particular ethnic or religious group, but for people who sense a kinship of values, who are prepared to work toward a future virtually unthinkable in the present.

Two girls, one Palestinian, one Jewish, are thinking about these things, whispering about them before they fall asleep at night, keeping themselves awake with ideas they have never shared with anyone else, sending notes back and forth when their teachers aren't looking. Have they invented a child's form of Arabrew, a

103

language in which secrets are kept? They do not want to be held back by what their teachers and parents think of as reality. They know that the desert can be made to bloom, that cities can be built in hot, windswept, arid settings. They know because these things are happening in their world.

One of their older sisters, who is studying city planning, has been filling their heads with plans she has seen for the creation of a city in the desert. It is called Masdar City, and it is down the road from Abu Dhabi in the United Arab Emirates. It will be a model ecological city, with 80 percent of its water recycled for use; it won't have cars; it will be run on power that comes from the sun. The water used for the crops will be collected underground and used all over again. Even the waste will be 100 percent recycled. This is not a dream for the future. Older sister has told them that it is already happening; the site has been selected and the building has begun.

The girls are less impressed than she has expected. They already know that the desert is just dry land waiting for water. They've heard of taking the salt out of seawater and diverting water from the Nile and bringing in water from a distance with pipes. They know the important thing is to get the fundamental ideas right and then let the details fall into place by themselves. They have both been to Neve Shalom/Wahat al-Salam. They have heard its story, and they are convinced you can make anything happen if you believe in it, if you take small steps and work hard.

Some of the problems their parents fret over do not seem troublesome to them. They have been friends since childhood, sleeping over at each other's homes, hanging out in the two different family circles. They take for granted that Arabs and Jews can live together. The Israeli girl has been listening to the grandmother of her Palestinian friend talk about the village where she grew up.

The old woman remembers their orchards and how the small children ran out every morning to see if the fruit was ripe. When she was little, grandmother could recognize from a distance the ripest fruit and get there first before anyone could stop her. She remembers the names of all her neighbors, of every person in the village and where they lived and how far the apple trees were from the houses. From this, the Israeli girl has decided that in their new world, people will build small villages. She knows the Palestinians are master builders, and she thinks it will be good for the Jews to work with their hands. Her Palestinian friend likes the stories she's heard about the early kibbutzim, especially the one where the Jewish grandmother lived. It belonged to a socialist movement, Hashomer Hatzair. The people there believed in egalitarianism between women and men and had always argued for the existence of a binational state. The disagreement between the girls about whether they should build villages or collective farms has been their first disagreement, easily enough resolved when it occurs to them that they can have both types of settlement; they can be each other's near neighbors and sleep over at each other's house. Neither of them wants to live in a big city, not even a city with solar power and recycled water. If cities have to be built for the people who want them they will leave that to older sister.

Where would their settlements be built? Obviously, in the Sinai. Lots of land, no people, people looking for a land. They have been told that Masdar City, with its narrow streets and shaded walks, is the pet project of an Arab sheik from the United Arab Emirates. He wants to do something he can really believe in. Maybe he has an older daughter who will want to make a contribution to peace in the Middle East? A few girls a little older than they are, from two or three oil-rich families, or maybe just from one rich family, can finance the project. The second cousin of the Jewish girl, who lives in New York, has come to Israel for his bar mitzvah. Everyone knows that when his grandfather dies he is going to inherit a lot of money. Both girls have been up late whispering with him. When other people hear about their project they will contribute. The girls know the formula: start small, work hard, be true to your vision and help will come. No profit is going to be made, no agencies will be involved, the organizations they need will form from the ground up. A just system of distribution of wealth will be found, and when they have problems they will all go together to Neve Shalom/Wahat al-Salam. Or maybe they will become their own Neve Shalom/Wahat al-Salam, another center where schoolchildren and older people can come to learn about conflict resolution and listening to one another. They think the children should all live together away from their parents; that way, if they want to stay up all night talking and making plans, there will be no one to interfere.

Who would want to go live in the New Sinai? It will be people whose homeland doesn't have to be something promised to them or even a place they think of as holy; people who are able to put aside their grief and pain over what has been taken from them. People who want to leave the bombings and curfews and checkpoints and identity cards and soldiers breaking into their houses any time of day or night, leave it all to anyone who wants to go on fighting over who came first and who has rights and who has suffered more, and who is more violent, and who has killed more of the other people. People who want to leave the whole mess behind because they want to start all over again, together.

One of these days they are going to write the whole thing up and read it to their class and find out if there is anyone who wants to join them. No one is going to listen to what their teachers have to say, or their parents, or the people who write books and articles in the newspaper and can't think of anything except the same old things nobody believes in. Peace conferences in Madrid, declarations of principles, Cairo agreements, Washington agreements, road maps. One of these days they will let everyone know what they are planning, and then all the children and older sisters and brothers who want to join them and any parents who think they will fit in and the grandmothers who won't have to walk, they can come along in cars and buses, will travel to every village and camp and city and small town and kibbutz and moshav and to the prisons and the hospitals and the schools and universities to spread the word.

Right now they are still whispering and passing notes in their own secret bilingual language, but all they have to do is stay friends and keep believing it can happen and grow up a little and the time will come.

The story has just begun.

11

Afterword: Must We Opine?

I used to be highly opinionated. It hasn't done me much good. Almost every opinion I held when I began this book I no longer hold. I had noticed, while writing, the tricky nature of "facts." Looked at more clearly, facts turned out to be opinions. My work done, I began to be aware of a problem with opinions. I found myself wondering whether it was necessary to have opinions. Then I wondered if statements that aspire to be opinions are usually something else.

"Opining" is an old-fashioned word. When it occurred to me, it made me laugh and brought to my attention that opining, having or speaking an opinion, is an active state; it involves some work, and may be a mental event still under consideration. Opining can be the act of *forming* an opinion.

An opinion, on the other hand, has an uncanny way of becoming part of one's identity; it grows into us, is hard to shake off. Even when we try to profess the subjective nature of an opinion *(well, it is only my opinion, but ...)* we have a sense that it is not only an opinion but something closer to a truth. A truth, indeed, that must on certain occasions be defended at all costs.

"Opining" describes a dynamic activity that might in the middle of constructing a sentence abruptly change its mind. As such, it shakes up the fixed and staid nature of an opinion, suggesting an activity that is much closer to thinking aloud than holding or holding on to an opinion. Have we abandoned this almost-lost verb because it no longer describes the way we have come to have and to hold opinions?

But even so, must we opine? Must we come to an opinion about everything? Can we tolerate a bit of uncertainty, a poised and dignified not-knowing? Is an opinion always and necessarily a partisan? And, if so, should there be preconditions for making a claim to having a right to have an opinion?

I recognize, of course, that there is no authority that can grant or withhold my right to an opinion, but I have developed some standards. To become an opinion, and to be regarded as such, any view I am entertaining must meet these criteria:

> It must know at least something about its subject matter.
> It must recognize that it is not a fact, a truth, or a certainty.
> It must be able to tolerate the presence of other opinions.
> It must become aware of its vested interests.

If it cannot rise to these conditions I will regard it as nothing more than a bias in need of scrutiny. I will not hold forth on it, proclaim it, or let it engage me in arguments; I will keep it to myself and make it do the work of self-reflection. How have I come to hold it? Why do I find it necessary? What would it cost me to let it go? What is there in it that makes me want to insist on its behalf?

These are, obviously, relevant questions for someone who has lost most of her previous opinions while still faced with tragic conflict in a part of the world that matters to her. I was surprised to discover as I was giving up opinions that nothing had changed in the world. I must have had the hope that an opinion was like an act taken, that a conversational victory over an opponent was crucial to the outcome of events in the Middle East. My opinions about how the struggle began, who was responsible for it, who keeps it going, who ought to admit to being wrong, who is justified or not in going to war, who ought to make reparations, who ought to be willing to receive them, and who is required to apologize were airy and not substantial. I gave up my opinions; things went on as they do. Civilians continued to suffer, men-at-arms continued to do violent and irresponsible things. The world did not seem to be in need of my opinions. Whatever they were, whether they changed or went missing, not the slightest puff of energy went forth to agitate the universe.

Do opinions—the making, having and holding of them—bring us any closer to the solutions we seek? And if not, why bother with them?

I realize that it is difficult to imagine going about without opinions. Suddenly, one feels naked, uncertain, not sure of who one is or what party one belongs to; the world seems ambiguous and complex and full of troubles for which there are no ready-made answers. Was it the Arabs or the Jews who began the war in 1948? *I have as yet no opinion. Tell me what you know about it. I'm willing to consider whatever you have to say.*

I also realize that I know very little about most of the things that have made me opinionated. I have ardently believed that the Israelis have the right to all the water they need. But what do I know about the origin of the water that flows into Israel? Was I ever really in a position to know if the Israeli army practices a purity of arms or if the IDF is the "only army in the modern world never to have dropped bombs indiscriminately on an enemy city?"[83] I have shouted and waved the two arms I have available, insisting that this is so. My shouting never made it so.

There are some things that escape from the limitation of being an opinion. To my mind it is not right to kill: not Jews, not Palestinians, not women who won't wear the veil nor their friends who go out dancing, not even the man who has murdered a child. This is not a question of having an opinion. It is a preference, and when it comes to being right or wrong, it is a belief.

And that, finally, is the problem with opinions. Most of them aren't opinions; they are too fixed and stubborn and insistent to deserve to be considered opinions. Most of them, and especially the ones causing most of the trouble, are necessary beliefs.

A belief is a very different creature than an opinion. One would never consider taking a belief through the rigorous standards I have evolved for opinions. A belief does not need to have knowledge of ascertainable things or gather information about its subject; we don't expect it to be tolerant of other beliefs, although we wish it could learn how; a belief believes in its certainty and, so far, no belief I have known ever became aware of its vested interest. We hold on to a belief because something in us would threaten to crack or break or disorganize without it. It had to be true that the Israeli Army practiced a purity of arms because my identity as a Jew demanded that I believe this. My identity went through a difficult time and survived, fully Jewish, although this belief has come into question and has ceased to be regarded as an opinion. Does the Israeli army practice a purity of arms? I am willing to opine about this, but I no longer hold it as a belief.

It would be helpful to distinguish opining from holding opinions and holding opinions from having beliefs. Beliefs like to disguise themselves as opinions, but beliefs are the trouble-makers. You do not kill an opponent because of an opinion. Opponents are murdered for their opposing beliefs.

Opining seems harmless enough. It doesn't conjure up two bull-like opponents with horns locked; it suggests people who would be able to stop their opining in order to listen to another's opining. Neither would have to have an opinion; together they are going over the information, examining its contradictions, weighing evidence, reflecting on it and inclining perhaps by the end of their discussion to a particular view, gently held, because it is, after all, only a view. If the view seems compelling enough, they might travel to the part of the world they've been talking about to see if there's anything they can do to help the people who are suffering there. Most of the people I know with strong opinions don't do much to change the way things happen on this earth. They tend to pace around, the way I used to, waving their hands and having their strong opinions. They too probably believe that this is equivalent to doing something meaningful in the world.

Must we opine? Yes, we must. And we must begin to teach our opinions whatever they can learn about opining.

Chronology

Chronologies are not what they seem: a straightforward, factual listing of events and dates.

A Palestinian writer noting the year 1948 is likely to say: War breaks out in Palestine. A characteristic entry from a Jewish writer: Israel attacked by Palestinian forces and the armies of surrounding Arab states.

For an entry on October 1973, Jewish writers will likely refer to the Yom Kippur War, implicitly emphasizing the outrage Jews felt when Israel was attacked on the holiest day of the Jewish calendar. A Palestinian writer will carefully note that the attacks occurred in occupied, Palestinian territory and will refer to the war simply as the 1973 War.

Population is one of the most contested issues in the history of Israel/Palestine. A Jewish writer would be likely to say that Palestine was underpopulated when the Jews of the first Aliyah arrived; a Palestinian writer would claim that an indigenous Palestinian people was displaced by the arrival of the Jews.

Same dates, same events, different stories.

When I reviewed this chronology, I discovered in every entry telltale signs of my bias as a Jewish writer. When I mention the hundreds of thousands of Arab Palestinians displaced by the war in 1948, I also include the hundreds of thousands of Jewish refugees from Arab countries. This seemingly straightforward juxtaposition is in fact a coded argument, implying some equality and justice in the exchange. A Palestinian reader would notice this slight-of-hand and contest it. On the other hand, in that same entry, I quote from Buber to remind readers of both peoples that some Jews refuse to blame the war and the aggression on the Palestinians.

I have included a chronology to help guide the reader through this long, complex, ever-changing story. But the guide is itself a highly selective way in which the story of dates and events is being told.

115

Aliyah, "going up," describes the immigration into Palestine by Jews. Those who "go up" are known as olim, *a biblical term used when the Children of Israel went up out of Egypt.*

1878–1904: First Aliyah. First wave of contemporary Jewish settlers, some 25,000 people, fleeing pogroms and anti-Semitism in Europe, arrive in Palestine and establish the first rural Jewish settlements.

1881: There are almost half a million Arabs living in Palestine, 90 percent of the population.

1904–14: Second Aliyah. Some forty thousand Jews immigrate to Ottoman Palestine, revive Hebrew as the language for Jews in Palestine, establish the kibbutz movement, the first Hebrew high school, and the city of Ahuzat Bayit, later renamed Tel Aviv. The Second Aliyah consists of young men and women, mainly from Russia, many of them socialists. They are inspired by the idea of building a workers' commonwealth and establish the first Jewish labor parties.

1914: There are 689,272 people living in Palestine, of whom 60,000 are Jews.

November 1917: Balfour Declaration. The British foreign secretary, Arthur James Balfour, writes to Lord Rothschild, president of the British Zionist Federation, stating that the British government views favorably the establishment of a national home for the Jewish people in Palestine.

December 9, 1917: General Edmund Allenby of the British army enters Jerusalem, ending four centuries of Ottoman rule of Palestine.

1919–22: Third Aliyah. Forty thousand Jews, most of them from Eastern Europe, arrive in Palestine. Although the British government imposes quotas on the Aliyah, there are some ninety thousand Jews in Palestine by the end of 1923. Tension increases between Arabs and Jews. Herbert Samuel, the British high commissioner, a Jew, pardons Jews and Arabs involved in the 1920 disturbances.

March 1922: Winston Churchill, then British colonial secretary, divides the Mandate of Palestine into two territories: Palestine, west of the Jordan River, and Transjordan, under the rule of the Hashemites. Jewish settlement is restricted to Palestine.

June 1922: The Churchill White Paper, the first official manifesto from the British government, clarifies the British position regarding the Balfour Declaration and the Palestine Mandate.

July 1922: The League of Nations assigns the British government as the mandatory for Palestine. The mandatory is to establish the Jewish national home and to safeguard the civil and religious rights of all the inhabitants of Palestine. Tension between Jews and Arabs continues to increase.

1922: There are 660,641 Arabs living in Palestine and 83,790 Jews. The population is 78 percent Muslim; 9.6 percent Christian (mostly Arab); and 11 percent Jewish.

1924–29: Fourth Aliyah. Some 82,000 Jews arrive in Palestine, fleeing anti-Semitism in Poland and Hungary. This group, artisans and shopkeepers of the middle class, settles in towns, largely in Tel Aviv, and invests in construction, small factories, shops, and restaurants. New agricultural villages are developed in the Coastal Plain. The Fourth Aliyah becomes popularly known as "the Grabski Aliyah," after the anti-Semitic Polish prime minister Wladyslaw Grabski.

April 1, 1925: Opening of the Hebrew University on Mount Scopus in Jerusalem.

Summer 1929: Riots between Jews and Muslims over access to the Wailing Wall, a remnant of the Jerusalem Temple. The Wall, part of the Western Wall, al-Buraq, is also holy to Muslims. Jewish communities are evacuated by the British from the Arab enclaves of Gaza and Hebron. These riots occasion a highly pessimistic mood in the Zionist movement, many of whose members are traumatized by the realization that the Zionist undertaking will be accompanied by violence.

1929–39: Fifth Aliyah. During the rise of Nazism in Germany, some 250,000 Jews arrive in Palestine.

October 1930: The Passfield White Paper, recommending limitation on Jewish immigration, causes a protest in the British parliament. The

League of Nations indicates that the restriction of Jewish immigration would put Britain in violation of its mandate to foster a national home for the Jewish people.

1934–48: *Ha'apalah:* the clandestine immigration of Jews to Palestine. In spite of restrictions imposed by the British, 115,000 clandestine immigrants arrive in Palestine.

May 1936–March 1939: Arab general strike. Arabs demand that Jewish immigration be stopped and that land not be sold to Jews. The Haganah, the Jewish defense organization, advocates restraint, but the Irgun, a Jewish terrorist organization, engages in retaliation. Some five thousand Arabs and four hundred Jews are killed.

July 1937: The Peel Commission recommends a partition plan, rejected by Arab leadership and, after much debate among the Jewish leadership, rejected also by the Twentieth Zionist Congress.

April 1938: The Woodhead Commission investigates new partition plans and finds that partition is not feasible.

May 17, 1939: A white paper proposing a unified Palestinian state imposes severe restrictions on Jewish immigration and the Jewish purchase of land.

1939: According to some statistics (all approximate) the Jewish population of Palestine, on the eve of World War II, numbers 475,000 people, 40 percent of the population.

May 1942: The Biltmore Program is formulated to oppose the strategy of the 1939 white paper. "The conference urges that the gates of Palestine be opened; that the Jewish Agency be vested with control of immigration into Palestine and with the necessary authority for upbuilding the country ... ; and that Palestine be established as a Jewish Commonwealth."

June 1942: Establishment of the League for Jewish-Arab Rapprochement and Cooperation. In August, the Ichud (Union) is established as a political party with an executive committee composed of Judah Magnes, Henrietta Szold, Gershom Scholem, and Martin Buber, among others. The Ichud favors a binational state and opposes the Biltmore Program.

November 29, 1947: The UN General Assembly passes Resolution 181 by a two-thirds majority. The partition plan recommends the division of the British Mandate of Palestine into two states and proposes to internationalize Jerusalem. The plan is accepted by Jewish leadership, rejected by Arab leadership.

November 1947: "Civil war" breaks out. Palestinian Arabs protest the UN partition plan.

April 9, 1948: Israeli forces attack the village of Deir Yassin. A number of Israeli historians regard this event as a massacre; although the number of civilians killed remains controversial, the Zionist Organization of America accepts the "low" number of 107, with a maximum of 120. Other accounts indicate 254 civilians killed.

May 14, 1948: Israel declares independence.

May 15, 1948: Arab-Israeli War, lasting thirteen months. Neighboring Arab states attack Israel. Hundreds of thousands of Arab Palestinians are displaced and scattered, creating the Palestinian refugee crisis. Hundreds of thousands of Jewish refugees from Arab countries flee to Israel. Martin Buber, in the journal *Be'ayot Ha-Yom,* argues that it would be disingenuous to claim that "we Israelis" are the innocent victims of Arab aggression.

December 11, 1948: UN General Assembly Resolution 194 states that "refugees wishing to return to their homes and live at peace with their neighbors should be permitted to do so."

1948: There are 1.35 million Arabs and 650,000 Jews living between the Jordan River and the Mediterranean Sea.

1948–56: Numerous cross-border encounters between Egyptian guerrilla and Israeli forces.

1949: Armistice agreements between Israel and neighboring Arab lands. Israel gains 77 percent of Palestine. The West Bank, including Old Jerusalem, comes under Jordanian rule and is later annexed by Jordan. The Gaza Strip is occupied by Egypt.

April 1949: Establishment of the new Hebrew journal, *Ner* (Light), intended to offer a nonpartisan forum that would alert the new State of Israel to the "evil" it might commit and to encourage its opportunities to advance justice.

October 29, 1956: Suez Crisis. France, Britain, and Israel join in the invasion of the Sinai Peninsula in response to Egypt's nationalization of the canal and its refusal to allow Israeli shipping.

May 1964: The Palestine Liberation Organization (PLO) is founded, with its stated goal the destruction of Israel. The PLO objects to Israel's plans to redirect water from the Sea of Galilee and the Jordan River for use in western Israel and the Negev Desert.

June 1967: Six-Day War. Israel defeats the armies of Egypt, Jordan, Syria, and Iraq and captures the Gaza Strip and the Sinai Peninsula from Egypt, the West Bank and East Jerusalem from Jordan, and the Golan Heights from Syria. The West Bank and Gaza are placed under military administration. Jews and Christians, previously forbidden entry under Jordanian rule, are now allowed to enter the Old City.

November 22, 1967: UN Security Council Resolution 242 demands the "withdrawal of Israeli armed forces from territories occupied in the recent conflict."

September 1968: Kiryat Arba is approved by the Israeli government as the first Israeli settlement in the West Bank.

February 1969: Yasir Arafat becomes chairman of the PLO.

1967–1970: "War of Attrition" between Israel and Egypt.

September 1970: The PLO is forced out of Jordan and driven into Lebanon.

1972: Founding of Birzeit University by Musa Nasir, with the intention to create a Palestinian version of the American University of Beirut.

April 9, 1973: Commando raid by Israeli forces against the PLO in Lebanon.

October 1973: Yom Kippur War. Syria and Egypt attack Israeli forces in the occupied Sinai Peninsula and the Golan Heights. Israeli forces rebuff the attack. The war lasts for sixteen days, after which UN Security Council Resolution 338 is passed, calling for international peace talks and affirming Resolution 242.

October 1974: The PLO is recognized by the Arab League as the representative of the Palestinian people.

April 13, 1976: The PLO wins municipal elections in the West Bank.

May 1977: Menachem Begin, the former leader of the Jewish terrorist organization Irgun, becomes Israeli prime minister after thirty years of governance by the left wing. Egyptian president Anwar al-Sadat visits Jerusalem and speaks to the Israeli Knesset. In return, Prime Minister Begin visits Ismailia.

September 17, 1978: Camp David Accords. Israel agrees to grant full autonomy to the Palestinians after five years of transition. Israel promises to stop Jewish settlement, but Jewish settlement continues in the West Bank and Gaza.

1978: There are 500 Jewish settlers in the Gaza Strip and 7,800 in the West Bank.

March 1979: Peace treaty between Israel and Egypt. Egypt recognizes Israel and ensures Israel's access to the Suez Canal; Israel withdraws from the Sinai.

July 1981: The PLO headquarters in Beirut is bombed by Israeli forces. The United States arranges a cease-fire between Israel and the PLO. Israel continues to establish settlements in the West Bank and Gaza. Egyptian president Anwar al-Sadat is assassinated.

1982: Lebanon War. Israel invades southern Lebanon. The PLO is driven out of Lebanon and forced into Tunis. Hezbollah, a militant Lebanese organization, regarded by Israel as a terrorist group, is established.

September 1982: Sabra and Shatila massacre by the Lebanese Phalange. Estimates regarding numbers of civilians killed range from 328 to 3,500, most estimates being in the thousands. Ariel Sharon, Israeli defense minister, who could have stopped the massacre, is held to be indirectly responsible by the Kahan Commission, which recommends his resignation. Sharon resigns.

August 1983: Withdrawal of Israeli army from Lebanon with the establishment of a safe zone in southern Lebanon.

1984: Continued establishment of Jewish settlements in Gaza and the West Bank, now including some eighty thousand settlers.

1985: Defense minister Yitzhak Rabin develops the "iron fist," a policy that sanctions deportation and detentions of the Palestinian population.

December 1987: First Intifada. The popular Palestinian uprising begins in the Jabalia refugee camp in Gaza and moves quickly to the West Bank. Israel responds with vigorous reprisal. Hamas, a militant Palestinian organization that denies Israel's right to exist, is established.

1988: Jordan gives up its rights in the West Bank and East Jerusalem to the PLO. Palestinian Declaration of Independence: first official Palestinian recognition of the legitimate existence of a Jewish state and endorsement by the PLO of a two-state solution.

July 1989: Magnetic cards are introduced by Israel in the occupied territories; the card becomes a requirement for leaving Gaza and working in Israel.

October 1991: Middle East peace conference in Madrid.

June 23, 1992: After fifteen years of Likud governance, Yitzhak Rabin and the Labor Party win the election with a sizable majority.

September 9, 1993: Israel and the PLO exchange Letters of Mutual Recognition.

September 13, 1993: The Declaration of Principles (Oslo Accords) is signed in Washington DC by the PLO and Israel. The PLO recognizes Israel's right to exist; Israel agrees to withdraw from parts of the West Bank and the Gaza Strip.

February 25, 1994: Baruch Goldstein kills twenty-nine Palestinians worshipping at the Ibrahimi Mosque, Hebron.

May 4, 1994: The Cairo Agreement establishes Palestinian self-rule in the Gaza Strip and Jericho.

May 17, 1994: Establishment of the Palestinian Authority. Jordan and Israel sign a peace agreement.

September 28, 1995: The Washington Agreement, also known as the Interim Agreement, is signed by Yitzhak Rabin, Yasir Arafat, and Shimon Peres, enhancing Palestinian self-rule. Palestinian autonomy is not permitted in areas intended for Jewish settlements.

November 4, 1995: Assassination of Yitzhak Rabin in Tel Aviv by Yigal Amir, a member of the religious right wing. Shimon Peres becomes acting prime minister.

January 20, 1996: Palestinian Legislative Council elections. Yasir Arafat is elected president.

February–March 1996: Suicide bombings in Jerusalem and Tel Aviv, claimed by Hamas, kill fifty-seven Israeli civilians and prompt closures of the Gaza Strip and the West Bank with severe administrative punishments by Israel. Palestinian workers are not allowed to return to work in Israel.

June 29, 1996: Election of Benjamin Netanyahu, leader of the right-wing Likud party, as Israeli prime minister.

September 2, 1996: A new bypass road opens between Jerusalem and the Etzion Bloc of settlements in the West Bank. The road serves to bypass Palestinian towns and divides Palestinian lands into separated cantons. The road has no checkpoint into Jerusalem and is forbidden to Palestinians from the West Bank.

1996: There are 150,000 Jewish settlers in the West Bank and Gaza, an increase of 49 percent since 1948, when the first settlement was established.

October 23, 1998: Yasir Arafat and Benjamin Netanyahu sign the Wye River Memorandum in Maryland, with President Bill Clinton as host.

July 2000: The Camp David Summit attempts to achieve a "final status" agreement between Israelis and Palestinians. Yasir Arafat declines a proposal made by Israeli prime minister Ehud Barak.

September 28, 2000: Ariel Sharon, with thousands of Israeli soldiers, visits the Temple Mount/Haram al-Sharif, Judaism's holiest and Islam's third-holiest site.

September 29, 2000: Second Palestinian Intifada.

January 2001: The Taba Summit peace talks seek to reach the "final status" negotiations. Ehud Barak withdraws from talks during the Israeli election.

February 6, 2001: Ariel Sharon, Israel's former defense minister, who resigned after the Sabra and Shatila massacre, is elected prime minister of Israel. Sharon, opposed to the Oslo Accords, declines to continue negotiations after the election.

February 2001: There are 205,000 Jewish settlers in the West Bank and Gaza, and 180,000 in East Jerusalem.

March 13, 2002: UN Security Council Resolution 1397 affirms the possibility of a two-state solution and calls for an immediate cessation to violence. Arafat, blamed by Israel for suicide bombings, is confined to his Ramallah office by Israeli forces.

April 12, 2002: Battle of Jenin. Israeli forces occupy a Palestinian refugee camp. Twenty-three Israeli soldiers are killed, along with fifty-two Palestinians, twenty-two of them civilians.

June 2002: Israel begins to construct a wall along the West Bank.

December 1, 2003: The Geneva Initiative (officially known as the Draft Permanent Status Agreement), an unofficial peace agreement between Israelis and Palestinians, is signed.

July 9, 2004: The West Bank wall is deemed illegal by the International Court of Justice; the UN considers the wall an act of annexation. This view is opposed by the United States, which regards the wall as a defense against terrorism.

November 11, 2004: Yasir Arafat dies.

September 12, 2005: Mahmoud Abbas (Abu Mazen) is elected president of the Palestinian Authority. Israel unilaterally disengages from the Gaza Strip and dismantles four settlements in the West Bank.

January 2006: Hamas wins the great majority of seats in the Palestinian legislature. Israel and the United States withhold funds to Palestinians. Ariel Sharon suffers a massive stroke.

March–August 2006: Ehud Olmert, elected Israel's prime minister, promises to continue building the separation wall. Hezbollah and Hamas capture Israeli soldiers; Israeli forces attack Lebanon and Gaza. The UN Security Council approves Resolution 1701. A fragile peace is established.

September 26, 2006: The humanitarian situation in Gaza is considered "intolerable" by the UN. Approximately 75 percent of Palestinians depend on aid for food; 80 percent live below the poverty line.

2006: The population of the Gaza Strip reaches about 1.4 million. The population of the West Bank reaches about 2.5 million.

November 13, 2008: There are 280,000 Jewish settlers in the West Bank and 200,000 Jews living in East Jerusalem. According to some statistics, half the settlers in the West Bank do not want to move back to Israel. Some 40 percent of them would be willing to return if a reasonable price were paid for their holdings.

For Further Reading

Hannah Arendt, *The Jew as Pariah: Jewish Identity and Politics in the Modern Age* (New York: Grove Press, 1978).

Naseer Aruri, ed., *Palestinian Refugees: The Right of Return* (London: Pluto Press, 2001).

Joel Beinin, *Was the Red Flag Flying There? Marxist Politics and the Arab-Israeli Conflict in Egypt and Israel, 1948–1965* (Berkeley: University of California Press, 1990).

Edwin Black, *The Transfer Agreement: The Dramatic Story of the Pact between the Third Reich and Jewish Palestine* (Washington: Dialog Press, 1999).

Martin Buber, *A Land of Two Peoples: Martin Buber on Jews and Arabs,* ed. Paul Mendes-Flohr (Chicago: University of Chicago Press, 2005).

Jimmy Carter, *Palestine: Peace Not Apartheid* (New York: Simon and Schuster, 2007).

Noam Chomsky, *Fateful Triangle: The United States, Israel and the Palestinians* (Cambridge, MA: South End Press, 1999).

Pauline Cutting, *Children of the Siege* (London: Pan Books, 1988).

Amos Elon, *The Israelis: Founders and Sons* (New York: Bantam Books, 1971).

Grace Feuerverger, *Oasis of Dreams: Teaching and Learning Peace in a Jewish-Palestinian Village in Israel* (New York: RoutledgeFalmer, 2001).

Simha Flapan, *The Birth of Israel: Myths and Realities* (New York: Pantheon Books, 1987).

Amira Hass, *Reporting from Ramallah: An Israeli Journalist in an Occupied Land* (Los Angeles: Semiotext(e), 2003).

Anne Karpf, Brian Klug, Jacqueline Rose, and Barbara Rosenbaum, eds., *A Time to Speak Out: Independent Jewish Voices on Israel, Zionism and Jewish Identity* (London: Verso, 2008).

Rashid Khalidi, *The Iron Cage: The Story of the Palestinian Struggle for Statehood* (Boston: Beacon Press, 2006).

Rashid Khalidi, *All That Remains: The Palestinian Villages Occupied and Depopulated by Israel in 1948* (Washington DC: Institute for Palestine Studies, 1992).

Rabbi Michael Lerner, *Healing Israel/Palestine: A Path to Peace and Reconciliation* (Berkeley: North Atlantic Books, 2003).

Rabbi Michael Lerner, *Jewish Renewal: A Path to Healing and Transformation* (New York: Harper Perennial, 1995).

Nur Masalha, *Expulsion of the Palestinians: The Concept of "Transfer" in Zionist Political Thought, 1882–1948* (Washington DC: Institute for Palestine Studies, 1992).

Nur Masalha, *The Politics of Denial: Israel and the Palestinian Refugee Problem* (London: Pluto Press, 2003).

Aaron David Miller, *The Much Too Promised Land: America's Elusive Search for Arab-Israeli Peace* (New York: Bantam Books, 2008).

Benny Morris, *1948 and After: Israel and the Palestinians* (Oxford: Clarendon Press, 1990).

Benny Morris, *The Birth of the Palestinian Refugee Problem Revisited* (Cambridge: Cambridge University Press, 2004).

Ilan Pappé, ed., *The Israel/Palestine Question: Rewriting Histories* (London: Routledge, 1999).

Edward W. Said, *The Politics of Dispossession: The Struggle for Palestinian Self-Determination, 1969–1994* (New York: Vintage Books, 1995).

Edward W. Said, *From Oslo to Iraq and the Road Map: Essays* (New York: Vintage Books, 2005).

Anita Shapira, *Land and Power: The Zionist Resort to Force, 1881–1948* (Stanford: Stanford University Press, 1999).

Raja Shehadeh, *The Third Way* (London: Quartet Books, 1982).

Eyal Weizman, *Hollow Land: Israel's Architecture of Occupation* (London: Verso, 2007).

Notes

Chapter 2

1. Martin Buber, *The Martin Buber Reader*, ed. Asher D. Biemann (New York: Palgrave-Macmillan, 2002), 146.
2. Amos Elon, "The Politics of Memory," *New York Review of Books*, October 7, 1993.
3. Nur Masalha, *The Politics of Denial: Israel and the Palestinian Refugee Problem* (London: Pluto Press, 2003), 56–57.
4. Ibid.
5. Ibid.
6. Ibid.

Chapter 3

7. Cited in Amos Elon, The Israelis, Founders and Sons (New York: Bantam Books, 1972), 362.
8. Ibid., 219.
9. Michael Prior, "The Right to Expel: The Bible and Ethnic Cleansing" in *Palestinian Refugees: The Right of Return,* ed. Naseer Aruri (London: Pluto Press, 2001), 9–35.
10. Edward Said: "There can be no conceivable peace ... that doesn't tackle the real issue, which is Israel's utter refusal to accept the sovereign existence of a Palestinian people that is entitled to rights over what Sharon and most of the people supporting him consider exclusively to be the land of Greater Israel, that is the West Bank and Gaza." (Edward W. Said, *From Oslo to Iraq and the Road Map,* New York: Vintage Books, 2005, 174.) Ariel Sharon: "But [we] believed without question that only [we] had rights over the land. And no one was going to force [us] out, regardless of terror or anything else. When the land belongs to you physically ... that is when you have power, not just physical power but spiritual power."

(Ariel Sharon, with David Chanoff, *Warrior: The Autobiography of Ariel Sharon*, New York: Simon & Shuster, 2001, 25.) (Tragedy, I think.)

11. Stefan Zweig, *The Royal Game* (New York: Viking Press, 1961), 9.
12. Raja Shehadeh, *When the Birds Stopped Singing: Life in Ramallah Under Siege* (Vermont: Steerforth Press, 2003), 78.
13. Bernard Avishai, *The Tragedy of Zionism: How Its Revolutionary Past Haunts Israeli Democracy* (New York: Helios Press, 2002), 150.
14. Geula Cohen, *Woman of Violence: Memoirs of a Young Terrorist, 1943-1948* (New York: Holt, Rinehart and Winston, 1966), 223.
15. Rashid Khalidi has written a finely reasoned, dispassionate account of the favoritism shown to the Zionists by the British during the first years of the mandate. I am not convinced that this colonial patronage in itself makes Zionism a colonial movement. I am, however, certain that this book should be read by anyone struggling to achieve an informed opinion on the question. Rashid Khalidi, *The Iron Cage: The Story of the Palestinian Struggle for Statehood*, (Boston, Beacon Press, 2006).
16. Edward W. Said, *From Oslo to Iraq and the Road Map: Essays* (New York: Vintage Books, 2005), 94.

Chapter 4

17. Sana Hassan, "Israel and the Palestinians," *New York Review of Books*, November 14, 1974.

Chapter 5

18. Dov Yermiya, *My War Diary: Lebanon June 5–July 1, 1982* (Boston: South End Press, 1999), 8.
19. Quoted in Yermiya, *My War Diary*, 149.
20. Benny Morris, *The Birth of the Palestinian Refugee Problem Revisited* (Cambridge: Cambridge University Press, 2004), 432–33.
21. Masalha, *Politics of Denial*, 39.
22. Said, *From Oslo to Iraq*, 11.

23. Ilan Pappé, *The Ethnic Cleansing of Palestine* (Oxford: One World, 2006), 9.

24. Masalha, *Politics of Denial,* 34.

25. Ibid.

26 Ibid., 35.

27. Alan Dershowitz, *The Case for Israel* (New Jersey: John Wiley and Sons, 2003), 68.

28. David Gilmour, *Dispossessed: The Ordeal of the Palestinians,* (London: Sphere Books, 1983), 97.

29. Dov Yermiya, *My War Diary* (Boston: South End Press, 1999), 113.

30. Raja Shehadeh, *Strangers in the House: Coming of Age in Occupied Palestine* (Vermont: Steerforth Press, 2002), 159.

31. *Hansard Parliamentary Debates,* Commons, 5th ser., vol. 861, col. 502, quoted in Gilmour, *Dispossessed,* 94.

32. Amos Elon, "The Jews' Jews," *New York Review of Books,* June 10, 1993.

33. Sana Hassan, "Israel and the Palestinians," *New York Review of Books,* November 14, 1974.

34. Yermiya, *My War Diary,* 32.

35. Said, *From Oslo to Iraq,* 93.

36. Elon, "The Jews' Jews."

37. Shehadeh, *When the Birds Stopped Singing,* 113.

Chapter 6

38. Sari Nusseibeh with Anthony David, *Once Upon A Country: A Palestinian Life* (New York: Farrar, Straus and Giroux, 2008), 199–200.

39. Ibid., 84.

40. Ibid., 87.

41. Yermiya, *My War Diary,* 134–35.

42. Fouzi al-Asmar, "The Impossible." In David Gilmour, *Dispossessed: The Ordeal of the Palestinians* (London: Sphere Books Limited, 1983), 91-92.

43. Gilmour, *Dispossessed,* 89.

44. Ibid., 81.

45. Ibid., 94.

46. Schlomo Shmelzman, letter to the editor, *Haaretz,* August 11, 1982.

47. Amira Hass, *Drinking the Sea at Gaza: Days and Nights in a Land Under Siege* (New York: Henry Holt, 1996), 55.

48. Ibid., 195.

49. Ibid., 154–55.

50. Ibid., 156.

51. Ibid., 56.

52. Ibid., 203.

53. Anita Shapira, *The Army Controversy, 1948: Ben-Gurion's Struggle for Control,* (Jerusalem: Hakibbutz Hameuchad Publishing House, 1985), 210.

54. Tom Segev, *1967: Israel, the War, and the Year that Transformed the Middle East,* (New York: Metropolitan Books, 2005), 409.

Chapter 7

55. David Shulman, *Dark Hope: Working for Peace in Israel and Palestine* (Chicago: University of Chicago Press, 2007).

56. Amos Elon, *The Israelis: Founders and Sons* (New York: Bantam Books, 1972), 215-16.

57. Shulman, Dark Hope, 32.

58. Ibid., 117.

59. Ibid., 66.

60. Ibid., 75.

61. Hass, *Drinking the Sea at Gaza,* 5.

62. B'Tselem, The Israeli Information Center for Human Rights in the Occupied Territories, http://www.btselem.org/English/index.asp.

63. Wendy Pearlman, *Occupied Voices: Stories of Everyday Life from the Second Intifada,* (New York: Thunder's Mouth Press/Nation Books, 2003), xxiv.

64. Amos Elon, "From the Uprising," *New York Review of Books,* April 14, 1988.

65. Shulman, *Dark Hope, 112.*

66. *Hass,* Drinking the Sea at Gaza, 54.

67. Ibid., 138.

68. Ibid., 140.

69. Ibid., 146.

70. Ibtisam Barakat, *Tasting the Sky: A Palestinian Childhood* (New York: Farrar, Straus and Giroux, 2007), 59.

Chapter 8

71. Avishai, *Tragedy of Zionism,* 249.

72. Peter Fritzsche, *Life and Death in the Third Reich* (Cambridge, MA: Belknap Press, 2008), 274.

73. Haim H. Cohn, *Human Rights in the Bible and Talmud* (Tel Aviv: Mod Books, 1989), 57.

74. Shulman, *Dark Hope,* 165.

75. Ibid., 121.

76. Nusseibeh, *Once Upon a Country,* 235.

77. Raja Shehadeh, *Palestinian Walks: Forays into a Vanishing Landscape* (New York: Scribner, 2008), 165.

78. Nusseibeh, *Once Upon a Country,* 286.

79. For information on the numerous historical languages of the Jews beyond Yiddish and Hebrew, see Harold Bloom, "The Glories of Yiddish" and "Rabbi Brenglass and the Massena Blood Libel," American Jewish Historical Society, Fall 2008, 11.

80. Yitzchok Levine, "An American Blood Libel—It Did Happen." *Hamodia,* October 7, 2008, English edition, C6.

81. Shulman, *Dark Hope,* 60–61.

Chapter 9

82. Grace Feuerverger, *Oasis of Dreams: Teaching and Learning Peace in a Jewish-Palestinian Village in Israel* (New York: RoutledgeFalmer, 2001).

83. Alan Dershowitz, *The Case For Israel* (Hoboken New Jersey, John Wiley & Sons, Inc. 2003) 150–151.

Index

About the Author

Kim Chernin's extensive body of work spans many genres, including fiction, nonfiction, and poetry, and is frequently concerned with Jewish themes. *Crossing the Border* explores life on a kibbutz in Israel, discussing memory, experience, and the inevitable dissimilarity between them. *In My Mother's House* tells the stories of four generations of Jewish women in Chernin's family. *The Flame Bearers* describes an ancient sect of Jewish women who inherit the necessity to pass on a sacred women's knowledge from generation to generation. Chernin's most recent novel is *The Girl Who Went and Saw and Came Back*. She lives in Northern California with her life companion, Renate Stendhal.